Teaching Children Language Arts

ROY R. WILSON, JR.

PARKER PUBLISHING COMPANY, INC., WEST NYACK, N.Y.

Dedication

To the memory of my grandmother, Louise Holtorf Wright, who is largely responsible for my love of language.

A Word from the Author About This Book

You are aware of the value that practical, imaginative ideas can bring to the classroom. The purpose of this book is to provide ideas of this type—directly related to language arts. The material will spark your own thinking, and because of that spark you will find yourself exploring new and exciting ways to do things through the magic of language arts. Thus, you will acquire specifics to try in the classroom as well as ideas to stir your own thinking toward a greater understanding of what needs to be done in the language arts classroom.

It is not enough just to teach a child how to acquire the skills. It is far more vital, after the child gains the skills necessary for reading, that he *does* read; and that he has some criteria by which to select what he will read, and finally, that he will know in his thinking processes what to *do* as a result of the things he reads. The child, after learning how to put pencil to paper and make marks that stand for words, must then have a *desire* to put words on paper, must have something to say, must believe that the written word is of value. The child needs to learn that his language is not just any sound dribbling out of the mouth or from the pencil, but that it is the basis through which ideas are expressed. We owe it to our children to help them in developing their own ideas and in understanding the ideas of others. The teacher has a basic responsibility that goes beyond teaching these skills. The skills are important. They must not be belittled. But they should not become the total program or any major part of the program. The teacher must excite children with the possibilities of making known the power of ideas. We have the responsibility of guiding children into the discovery of this fascinating world of our language. This is what makes us what we are, taking us into a world all other animals cannot enter or enjoy. Man is his language. Because man is able to read, write, listen, speak, and think, he has the potential for being something far beyond any other animal on earth. Whether he meets or strives to meet his potential is dependent upon the quality and variety of the experiences we as teachers and as fellow human beings allow children to have with language.

The first part of the book deals with the oral-listening phases of language arts. Since so much of our life from the very beginning is spent in hearing and in speaking it seems appropriate to begin the book here. The second part of the book then moves on into the area of writing. Throughout the oral, listening, and writing sections of the book I will frequently suggest ways to use our wealth of children's literature, for a great deal of the material here will be based upon the use of good literary selections, those read aloud and those that children read to themselves. Outstanding literary models should serve as a useful guide in helping the child to make use of his language more effectively.

This book takes up where most texts end, for it is customary to provide teachers with books which can be used to teach children *how* to read, spell, and write. Yet, when it comes to stimulating original experiences with the language, teachers express a continuing need for fresh ideas and help in motivating their students to *use,* in productive and creative ways, the skills that are being learned.

Each chapter contains creative suggestions for ways in which children can use the reading, writing, and speaking skills they have been taught. Most chapters include a bibliography, and there is a more extensive one in the final chapter. Thirteen of the chapters contain a plan for a bulletin board as well as specific comments for its most effective use. The bulletin boards are intended to be functional, not merely decorative, and can do much to increase the creative potential in your classroom for meaningful language arts experiences.

Roy R. Wilson, Jr.

Acknowledgments

For help in preparing this manuscript and for inspiration in my teaching I am indebted to: Mildred Hoyt Bebell, Hazel Dunnington, Sara Fenwick, Louise Lampman, Alberta Munkres, Zena Sutherland, and Dale Wile.

I also am grateful to my wife, Thelma, for her assistance in the early task of typing a preliminary copy from my very rough longhand notes.

Mr. Merwyn L. Mullins performed a superb service in translating my crude ideas for bulletin boards into the illustrations included in this volume.

And finally, acknowledgment is made to the following authors and publishers for permission to reprint selections from copyrighted material:

Atheneum Publishers for permission to reprint the poem "A Yell for Yellow" from *There Is No Rhyme for Silver* by Eve Merriam. Copyright © 1962 by Eve Merriam.

Bobbs-Merrill Company, Inc. for permission to quote several sentences from *Benjamin West and His Cat Grimalkin* by Marguerite Henry, 1947. Illustrated by Wesley Dennis.

Wm. Collins Sons & Co. Ltd. for permission to reprint the poem "Washing" from *More About Me* by John Drinkwater.

Pearl Riggs Crouch of Ashland, Oregon for permission to reprint her poem "A Story in the Snow."

Grade Teacher Magazine for permission to reprint the poem "A Halloween Chant" by D. Matthews and the poem "Joe's Snake Story" by Ruth Eckman. Harcourt, Brace & World, Inc. for permission to reprint a selection from *The White Archer* by James Houston, 1967.

Helen Herford of Nye, Montana, for permission to reprint the poem "The Elf and the Dormouse" by Oliver Herford.

Houghton Mifflin Company for permission to reprint the poem "Grizzly Bear" from *The Children Sing in the Far West* by Mary Austin.

The Instructor Magazine for permission to reprint "Blueprint for a Story" by Leona C. Karr published March 1967, page 32. Copyright The Instructor Publications, Inc.

J. B. Lippincott Company for permission to reprint the poem "The Goblin" from *Picture Rhymes from Foreign Lands* by Rose Fyleman. Copyright 1935, 1963 by Rose Fyleman.

David McKay Company, Inc. for permission to reprint a selection from *The Barrel* by Ester Wier. Copyright © 1966 by Ester Wier.

W. W. Norton & Company, Inc. for permission to reprint the poem "What the Wind Said" from *The Pedaling Man and Other Poems* by Russell Hoban. Drawings by Lillian Hoban. Text copyright © 1968 by Russell Hoban. Illustrations copyright © 1968 by Lillian Hoban.

The Viking Press for permission to reprint a selection from *Travels with Charley in Search of America* by John Steinbeck, 1962.

THE AUTHOR

Contents

3. Involving Students in Classroom Discussions *(Continued)*

cussion leaders · An experiment in student-directed discussion · Procedures for evaluation · Planning for future discussions

Three aspects: vocabulary, pronunciation, and usage · Is the way you talk bad? · Our language is losing its richness · Ways to become familiar with dialects

Let's begin with sharing time · Effective sharing demands appropriate teacher reactions · Where to begin more formal talks by children · What to consider when giving prepared oral talks · Procedures for evaluation

Variations for the primary-aged child · Ways to approach choral reading with older children · Suggested material for choral reading · Dangers to be alert to · Procedures for evaluation

There is a difference between hearing and listening · Do students and teachers listen? · Suggestions for becoming more effective listeners · How to measure listening ability

**12. Guidelines to Effective Nonfiction Writing
(Continued)**

*Writing a book—what it takes to do "re-
search" · Writing letters, real ones · Keeping
journals · A school newspaper at any grade*

*The need to have ideas to express before skills ·
The problems presented by spelling, punctuation, and grammar · Spelling · Punctuation
and grammar · Proofreading*

*NCTE—your professional organization · Files
of all sorts · Other materials you need in the
classroom · Annotated bibliography · Suggested list to send home to parents who want
ideas about books to read aloud*

1

How to Bring Children and Good Books Together

Essential foundation for building communication skills

Children who have access to good books are well on their way to developing meaningful and powerful language facility. Hopefully the children you teach will have books at home as well as parents who find time regularly to read. Realistically, you know many of the children in your classroom will discover books only through your efforts. Your classroom must reflect your belief in the value of books. There needs to be a variety of books available in the classroom, variety both in content and readability level.

You will reflect the belief you have in the importance of the role of books in children's lives when the following conditions exist: the books in your classroom are periodically changed, trips to the school library are regularly scheduled, bulletin boards are planned attractively to "sell" specific books (don't let a bulletin board get old and faded; if you believe that books are alive and exciting, change this board more frequently than any other bulletin board), time is taken to share together the books that have been read recently, and, most important, if your students observe *you* reading. Have at your desk an adult book of fiction or nonfiction that you obviously are eager to read. If reading really is important, then children should see

11

the adults, who say it is, actively and regularly involved in genuine reading. There is a temptation to believe that unless you are checking papers, planning lessons, and conferring with students rather than taking time to sit silently at your desk engrossed in a book, you are failing in your responsibility to the children. I am convinced one's living example that reading must happen will do far more in meeting one's responsibility to the educational needs of the students.

Reading aloud to children is a must

Another valuable way of bringing children and good books together is by reading aloud to the class regularly. This is not an activity that should be considered a treat for Friday afternoon, nor one to withhold as a disciplinary measure. Have you ever said, "If the class does not behave, or cooperate, there will be no arithmetic today"? As part of the daily curriculum, reading aloud should be considered as important as the other subjects, even arithmetic. Children should not have to earn the right to hear good literature.

What should happen when children are read to?

There are two major purposes for reading aloud to children on a daily basis. The first is to acquaint children with the many moods and qualities of our language. You may wish to read the book ahead of time in order to get the overall "feel" of the story, its action, the personalities of the characters, and the flow of the language. All teachers can have success in reading aloud if they believe in the value of this activity and have a genuine concern to communicate the excitement, humor, and conflict of the story to the children. Each oral reading is practice for the next. I have observed my own growth in reading aloud effectively over the many years of regular, daily reading to children. There is an intimate joy in sharing a good book together this way.

Bringing children together with good books is the second major purpose for teachers to read to children. By careful selection you open the doorways to the wide varieties of excellent books that have been written for children, and in this way you may stimulate children to further develop their reading skills. For those children who find learning to read a difficult and near-meaningless task, the read-aloud period may motivate new interest and result in future reading success.

Help for the teacher in deciding what books to read aloud

I plan my literature program for the year very carefully. In 1948 there were less than 1,000 books published yearly for children. Today there are close to 3,000 titles annually. Thus, selecting the few books you can read in a school year becomes a very serious matter. I am eager to introduce a variety of books in order more successfully to reach most of my students and to introduce types of stories and authors many children might not otherwise meet.

Each teacher will develop his own collection of books for a rewarding yearly literature program, and considerations for the age level of the children, their specific interests, and the experiences (or lack of experiences) will help in the decision of the books that are chosen for reading aloud. Let me suggest some of my preferences and state my reasons for them, as the reasons may serve to guide you in your choices.

To begin the year I usually have chosen a mystery because it allows for suspense, and in this way I establish myself as someone who loves a good story and wants to share it. Then, too, a mystery usually has chapters that end "up in the air," so that each day's reading leaves the children eager for more. I have had excellent success with Phyllis Whitney's *Mystery of the*

Black Diamonds [1] with children in grades 3 through 6. This mystery is about a ghost town, so there are exciting passages where my voice can relay the eerie feeling that the protagonists are in a deserted town that is still inhabited by *something*. Miss Whitney also handles a problem of prejudice with sensitivity, and so I am able, in the presentation of an exciting mystery, to deal appropriately with feelings young people may have when they are confronted with prejudice.

A favorite of mine, and one all children (as well as adults) should know is *Charlotte's Web* by E. B. White.[2] This book has joyous humor and genuine pathos. It is a beautifully written book about loyalty, and it deals honestly but gently with the joy of life and realism of death. Again, I have used it in grades 3 through 6. In recent years I have found more and more children know *Charlotte's Web* when they come to me, but after reading it to a group of fifth graders who all had heard it in third grade, I realized the power this book has. It is a book one can read many times, and each time it has something refreshing to say to the reader. I am reluctant to repeat a book children already know for there are so many books to introduce to children, but Charlotte's story is one I gladly repeat.

I generally choose books that will appeal to the boys, for I have found such books usually hold the girls' interest, but seldom do books written especially for girls suit the boys in the audience. One exception is Kate Seredy's *The Good Master*.[3] This book tells a delightful story of a tomboy who comes to live with her boy cousin and his parents in rural Hungary. My main reason for choosing the book, besides the fact that it is such a good story, is the strong characterization of the father-figure. It is important to present children with stories that portray strength in the father character. There are not enough of these books, and all children need to be able to identify with posi-

---

[1] Phyllis Whitney, *Mystery of the Black Diamonds* (Philadephia: Westminster Press, 1954).

[2] E. B. White, *Charlotte's Web,* illustrated by Garth Williams (New York: Harper & Row, 1952).

[3] Kate Seredy, *The Good Master* (New York: Viking, 1935).

tive and honest characterizations of loving fathers. *The Good Master* has been successful in grades 4 through 6.

A book that has strong appeal for boys is *My Side of the Mountain* by Jean George.[4] It has received wide acceptance in grades 3 through 6. The story is about a 16- or 17-year-old city boy whose understanding family allows him to spend a year in the wilds of the Catskill Mountains. His experiences in learning to deal with the elements are carefully detailed. This book is effectively used prior to or during a school camp activity or a unit on conservation.

A charming satire that has been enjoyed by fourth- through sixth-grade listeners is Jean Merrill's *The Pushcart War*.[5] The humor can be enjoyed on several levels, so this is another book that readers can return to and find stimulating.

A story that seems just right in the cold winter months with snow and ice lingering on for days and weeks is *Far Out the Long Canal* by Meindert deJong.[6] It tells of a boy in the Netherlands who is in fourth grade and has not yet learned to ice skate because the last real freeze, which was four years ago, lasted only one week, the week he was sick with pneumonia while all the other first graders were learning to skate on the canal. It is a story of strong, positive family relationships and of the real temptations a boy can yield to, with the resulting unpleasant consequences. This book should appeal to grades 3 through 6. It stands oral reading beautifully.

Another deJong book I have read to fourth, fifth, and sixth graders is *The House of Sixty Fathers*.[7] There are very few suitable books about war for young children: this one handles the subject with sufficient realism but maintains an appropriate tone for children. War is a subject that today's children, because of

---

[4] Jean George, *My Side of the Mountain* (New York: Dutton, 1959).

[5] Jean Merrill, *The Pushcart War*, illustrated by Ronni Solbert (New York: W. R. Scott, 1964).

[6] Meindert DeJong, *Far Out the Long Canal*, illustrated by Nancy Grossman (New York: Harper & Row, 1964).

[7] Meindert DeJong, *The House of Sixty Fathers*, illustrated by Maurice Sendak (New York: Harper & Row, 1954).

television, movies, and newspapers, cannot avoid. *Sixty Fathers* does a superb job of presenting the very human elements that survive even war.

Usually I end the year with *The Real Book of George Washington Carver* by Harold Coy.[8] I want to read a biography, and this is a well-written one for children in grades 3 through 6. I also want to read a story that deals with the racial problems our society must face. Harold Coy has handled the struggle which the Negro Carver faced throughout his life without sentimentality or didacticism. A third reason I choose this book is to read about a true American who was committed to something far more significant than making money, who had a deep, personal, social, scientific involvement.

For children prior to third grade there is a host of outstanding books, usually referred to as picture books, that can be carefully selected for oral reading. Incidentally, the best of the picture books should also find their way into the literature period of older children. I often introduce new ones to fifth and sixth graders by saying, "Here are some books that have been published since you were in the primary grades, and they are too good to miss." I also appeal to the outstanding, imaginative art work as a justification for sharing picture books with older children.

Ezra Jack Keats' books *Snowy Day* [9] and *Whistle for Willie* [10] handle the racial element without even mentioning it, but rather in the illustrations. One story captures the joy of the first snowfall, and the other presents a satisfying solution to a common wish of young children, how to succeed in whistling.

Where the Wild Things Are by Maurice Sendak [11] tells of a naughty boy who escapes into an exotic dreamland for a time,

---

[8] Harold Coy, *The Real Book of George Washington Carver*, illustrated by Elinor Blaisdell (New York: Franklin Watts, 1951).

[9] Ezra Jack Keats, *The Snowy Day* (New York: Viking, 1962).

[10] ———, *Whistle for Willie* (New York: Viking, 1964).

[11] Maurice Sendak, *Where the Wild Things Are* (New York: Harper & Row, 1963).

and then decides to return home where he finds an understanding mother who has brought him something to eat after he was sent to bed without supper.

May I Bring a Friend? by Beatrice Schenk deRegniers [12] tells of a boy's relationship with two adults who willingly accept each and every one of his most unusual friends.

Whatever books you choose to read aloud, be sure to know your reasons for selecting them. Turn for help in finding new books each year to such excellent reviewing aids as the *Bulletin for the Center of Children's Books* and to *Horn Book*. Remember that *you* need variety, so each year choose several books you have never read aloud before and set aside some you have reread many times. Occasionally during the year bring in a stack of books and "tease" the children's interests by simply reading the first chapters, then ask for volunteers to take the books for silent reading. One year I did this, using a special marker, so that when a child finished the book and returned it to me I would read aloud another chapter, then offer it again. When it came back I read another chapter, then offered it to yet another interested reader. In this way I actually read several complete books to the class, and at the same time many of the children were able to read the books themselves.

One other point when selecting books for reading aloud: include some poetry, both from anthologies and from single poets. John Ciardi's *The Reason for the Pelican* [13] and Eve Merriam's volumes *It Doesn't Always Have to Rhyme* [14] and *Catch a Little Rhyme* [15] are quite charming to share. When you read poems to children it is best to read each poem twice, once to introduce it and once to help them savor the beauty of the words.

---

[12] Beatrice Schenk DeRegniers, *May I Bring a Friend?* Illustrated by Beni Montresor (New York: Atheneum, 1964).

[13] John Ciardi, *The Reason for the Pelican,* illustrated by Madeleine Gekiere (Philadelphia: Lippincott, 1959).

[14] Eve Merriam, *It Doesn't Always Have to Rhyme,* illustrated by Malcolm Spooner (New York: Atheneum, 1964).

[15] ———, *Catch a Little Rhyme,* illustrated by Imero Gobbato (New York: Atheneum, 1966).

What to do when children bring books from home for you to read aloud

Be firm. Be friendly. But refuse. If you are carefully selecting books to share with your class you cannot afford to be diverted by these contributions from home. Often the books from home are not of enough literary quality, and they tend to force you to dwell on topics you have already presented. Your responsibility is to introduce children to a wide variety of literature, not to go into depth in any one area. How often after I have read an excellent horse story such as Marguerite Henry's *King of the Wind* [16] do I get a deluge of "favorite" horse stories from home to read to the class. My answer: "It's good of you to want to share your book with us Tell us a little about it, and then we will make a special place for it where other children can check it out. I won't be able to read it to the class, for I have chosen a number of books that children also like to hear, and it will be difficult to get them all read this year." I hope I do not hurt any child's feelings, but I do want my students to know that the literature period is as well planned by me as any other part of the school curriculum and that I choose specific books to read aloud for specific purposes.

With the primary children I would be much less likely to refuse any child's offering. Such books are usually the kind that can be completed in one short reading, and at this age I would do all I could to encourage such enthusiastic interest. Even so, I have my doubts about giving time to reading some of the mediocre supermarket-type fare that young children bring. So I would do all I could to surround young children with the best of the available picture books.

---

[16] Marguerite Henry, *King of the Wind* (Chicago: Rand McNally & Co.).

How to keep the reading-aloud period from becoming a literature-analysis period

For all the grand purposes one has in reading specific books aloud, the important thing is to "capture" children with a good story. One must be careful about interrupting a good story to enunciate other purposes, no matter how worthwhile. Interruptions must be kept at a minimum. When I read *Charlotte's Web* I pause only long enough to point out to the children how successful Mr. White is in taking you from very serious thoughts right into extremely humorous situations. What White has to say about loyalty and death I let him say in his own effective prose. I do not need to hammer away at it.

When a book is done I let the children talk about it as they wish. My comments are directed merely to get the children's reactions, not to put my ideas into their heads. Good books should be able to stand on their own, and thus they will communicate to each listener according to his readiness to receive the values and appeals of any particular book.

When I want to use examples of a writer's style to help guide children in their own writing I do that at another time during the day, not in the literature period. There are many possibilities in using samples from good literature to encourage children in their own writing, and these we will look at in later chapters.

Children need time to read to themselves

Once many years ago I finally realized that in my frenzy to teach reading to the usual three groups, which always worked out to be four in my classroom, I was forgetting the primary purpose for reading instruction, mainly that students *will* read. All of the workbooks, basal reader activities, and worksheets were for naught if there was no time simply to read. And so I began introducing the idea to my students each September that there definitely would be time every day for each child to read in books of his own choice, and I went on to say that in my classroom there should never be the comment, "I'm all finished with my work and I don't know what to do now." Each child must always have a library book in his desk available to read whenever he has finished with his work or is waiting for help from the teacher.

A most effective time for me to set aside for free reading has been the opening 15 to 30 minutes of each morning. I have established with my students the idea that when they arrive at school and have taken care of such things as purchasing lunch tickets, sharpening pencils, and preparing other school materials, they should get out their library books and start reading. To provide an environment appropriate to this activity I have some pleasant orchestral music playing on the phonograph and, most important, I am engrossed in a book. This means that I must be well enough organized so that I do not spend that first half-hour of the morning preparing lessons, checking papers, or taking lunch count. In grades 3 through 6 I have taught children in September to sign in on a dittoed attendance sheet and to indicate lunch or milk orders on the same form. Most of the children take turns tabulating and sending the correct order and attendance to the office. This has relieved me of the distracting responsibility of morning duties so that I can practice what I am preaching: reading is important; I do it; there are not enough hours in my life to do all the reading I want to do.

Another benefit of starting the day with silent, free reading is that it is a settling activity, one that promotes a classroom under control. Some mornings it is so silent and we are all so involved in our personal reading that time slips away. There have been mornings when I realize we have spent close to an hour "lost in books."

The silent reading period is such an essential part of the school day that I have disciplined myself never to say to the principal when he stops by, "Oh, yes, you can interrupt us.

We're just reading." *Just* reading! No, my answer is, "Can you come back sometime when we are talking or active. This is a bad time to interrupt for we are reading." Do all you can to convince everyone from the administration to the parents to your students that reading is an activity of top priority.

Ways for children to share the books they read

Children want to share the books they have read with others, and they should. Such sharing serves to stimulate all of us to go on reading. Children should know many ways to tell others about the books they have read which made an impression. Examples of many ways of sharing can be displayed at the beginning of the school year, and if materials are made accessible, children should be encouraged throughout the year to use their own time to prepare book presentations.

Here are some suggested ways in which children can prepare book sharings independently:

1. BOOK JACKETS
construction paper, crayons, and paint

Show commercial book jackets. Stress that the cover picture should capture a "big idea" from the book. Read various blurbs from the flaps. Suggest that information about the author or quotes from actual reviews might go on the back—this will lead children to read reviews that should be available in the library.

2. PEEP BOXES
old shoe boxes, scrap construction paper, pipe cleaners for figures, glue, cotton for snow and clouds, scraps of sponge or styrofoam for trees and shrubs

Children can write brief explanations on a card which then is placed on the table in front of the box scene. This can also be fun for a whole class to do after you finish reading a book aloud. After the scenes are constructed, everyone can guess which episodes from the book have been depicted by the different students.

3. Stick Puppets

*lath strips about 2 feet long, construction paper, cardboard,
glue*

Cut out characters twice, once in construction paper and once in cardboard. Glue the two together and then glue to end of sticks. These puppets have the advantage of simplicity in the making, therefore they do not require too much time. A desk or table can be used for a stage. The cardboard gives the puppet some durability.

4. Oral Talks

Children of all ages can prepare something to tell about the books they have read. Encourage a *variety* of ways to talk about a book: (*a*) the story up to a point, then tell others to read the book to find out what happens; (*b*) one specific episode in the book; (*c*) tell the entire story. This is a fine oral language arts activity. Children should have opportunities to tell stories to an audience.

5. Illustrations

butcher paper, manila paper, crayons, and paint

A child can prepare a bulletin board with a series of pictures about the book. Also, a series of pictures can be mounted on a long roll of paper and attached at each end to a round stick. The sticks can be placed in a cardboard box so that the picture story can roll by as a television or movie show. Another way pictures can be shared is to make a booklet which also includes some text on each page.

These are all independent activities, and children should be urged to create original ways to share books with the class.

There are a number of activities for sharing books that can be developed in class with your guidance. These activities bring into action various useful language arts experiences, and they also may help children to have a fuller understanding of the ideas in the books they have read. The following suggestions are especially useful when most of the children have read the same book (now that many of the fine books for children are available in paperback, it is possible to have duplicate copies in the classroom for very little expense):

1. ROUND TABLE

If a group of four or five have recently read the same book, the rest of the class can learn from a round table discussion. The participants should sit together in the front of the classroom, preferably around a table. They should have copies of the books with them. Some of these discussions should include you as a participant (only if you have read the book recently!) for you can, by example, guide children through fruitful discussion and thus establish a suitable pattern for future discussions when you should be a member of the audience, not a participant. Tape recording these discussions can provide excellent material for various kinds of evaluations and for the basis of other oral language activities.

Suggested guide questions for Round Table

For primary—

a) Did ___(main character)___ do things that children you know really do?
b) How do you feel about animal characters who talk?
c) How did the pictures help you enjoy the story?
d) Why do you think ___(specific character)___ did ___(specific)___ ?

For intermediate—

a) How did the author get across a mood of humor, suspense, action?
b) Did ___(main character)___ really solve his problem(s) or did someone or something else actually do the solving?
c) What examples of dialogue seem true? What are some samples of artificial dialogue?
d) How effective is the author in helping you picture certain scenes?

2. OTHER DISCUSSIONS

When most or all have read the same book, whole class discussion can get at deeper understandings of the book. Such discussion is appropriate after you have finished reading a book aloud to the class. The same guides as suggested for the round table will be effective here. You can also do more with specific samples for discussion. You might want to concentrate on the author's choices of adjectives or his use of verbs. You also could discuss reasons why the story began where and when it did. Another point for discussion is the author's choice of chapter titles. Another topic might be on the success of the author in developing fairly complete, though subordinate, characters.

3. DRAMATIZATION

A story that has moved a class has possibilities for dramatization. More will be said about this in the next chapter.

4. CREATIVE WRITING

Children can compare similar or dissimilar stories. They can write a comparison of specific characters from two different books or of the ways two authors describe similar settings. There is also merit in having some children try to write a story or description or opinion from the point of view of certain characters who appear in a book they have read.

5. PREPARED READINGS FOR OTHER CHILDREN

One of the most delightful and rewarding experiences is for children to go to other classrooms and read aloud to a new audience. An especially effective experience is to have children prepare something to read to children of another age. Primary youngsters who are excited by their newly-learned skill of reading can find some very receptive ears in the intermediate grades. Older children enjoy the genuine pleasure they can bring to very young children by reading them stories. A most appropriate way for expediting this experience is to work in small groups. All children should have an opportunity to volunteer, both as readers and as listeners. This is an especially good way for older children who find great difficulty in reading to have beneficial experiences reading "easy" books to younger children. Of course, even the most able students will learn from and enjoy this type of activity. I have had fourth, fifth, and sixth graders take small groups of kindergarten children once each week to the school library. Sometimes they browse with the younger ones, reading several books aloud together; other times the older children prepare a story to read; and at times the older children prepare a story to tell. At each library period they help the young children check out new books and return those that were borrowed previously. With the aid of the librarian I conduct an evaluation session following each period. The older children discuss the problems of selecting suitable stories and of having success in communicating with the younger children. I recall watching a fifth-grade boy in the library rapidly reading through a picture book, his full attention on the text of each page. What he could not see was the five-year-old boy sitting next to him looking about the room and paying no attention to the reader or to the story. In the evaluation session I pointed out the need to involve the listener by frequently looking at him, by commenting on some of the illustrations, and by drawing comments from him.

Pupil-teacher conferences about books

Conferences with individual children concerning the books they have read are worth the time they demand, and they *do* take time. There are at least six desirable outcomes of such conferences:

1. Both teacher and child gain better ideas about books the child might read in the future.
2. The child may come to see a relationship between himself and some character in the book. This does not mean the child has to have the same feelings or experiences (though this could happen), but, rather, the child understands both himself and the character in the book, even if they happen to be opposites, better than before his acquaintanceship with the book.
3. Ideas for creative writing, for dramatizations, and for discussions are explored.
4. Child comes to recognize the worth of his opinions and can feel comfortable in expressing ideas that are different from those of the teacher.
5. Vocabulary growth may occur.
6. Teacher broadens his understanding of the child's world. (It's easier to forget childhood than you may realize!)

Points a teacher might follow in a pupil-teacher conference based on books the child has read or heard:

1. Ask "why" questions.

   a) Why did a character say what he did in a specific situation?
   b) Why did a character do what he did in a specific situation?
   c) Why did the author write this story? (For more mature, older readers.) Or, what is the "big idea" of this story?

2. Ask questions that call for comparisons:

   a) Between characters.
   b) Between characters and the child (also people he knows).
   c) Between settings of the story and real life.
   d) Between happenings of the story and happenings in real life.

3. Ask questions that grow out of answers to preceding questions.
4. Suggest other specific books for child to read, based on data gathered from conference.
5. Explore meanings of words and phrases.
6. When possible, explore an opinion that may be contrary to child's opinion. Try to justify your opinion, but also encourage the child to have differing opinions. Hopefully, the child will feel free enough to justify his ideas, too.

It is difficult to schedule time with each child for conferences during the year, but they are necessary if we are to make reading a meaningful, productive experience. A realistic goal could be four conferences with each student during the year. Some of your most effective teaching is likely to occur during these individual conferences. Make it a practice to keep an anecdotal record of each conference. This record will aid you in subsequent evaluations, parent conferences, and future planning.

IN SUMMARY

1. Teachers must be an example of those who believe reading is important, and they must take time to read *in the presence of children.*
2. Reading aloud to children should occur regularly and never be regarded as a treat to be earned.
3. Oral reading to children brings books alive and is a dynamic way to introduce new kinds of books to children.
4. Careful selection is necessary in choosing books to read aloud. Stories that deal with social values, parent and peer relationships, and emotional values need to be included.
5. Avoid analysis of literary works. Let students be free to respond, but unless they initiate comments, allow the quality of the literature to stand on its own.
6. Recognizing the great concern to teach children *how* to read, remember that time must also be provided daily *to* read, in books selected by the children.
7. Encourage students to share with others the books they have

read but let much of the planning and preparation be done outside of class. If you have extra class time it should be spent *in reading.*

8. Consider the value of holding individual conferences to discuss books that have been read.

Bibliography

Bulletin for the Center for Children's Books. Published by the University of Chicago Press for the Graduate Library School. It is issued monthly except for August. It is a much needed resource as it evaluates current books for children on a scale from "recommended" to "not recommended." The reviews are discriminating and include suggested age level use.

Horn Book. Published in Boston. It is issued six times a year. Books reviewed in this periodical are considered by the editors and reviewers as fine literature.

Saturday Review. Once each month there is a column devoted to children's books. The opening remarks of Zena Sutherland, the editor, give valuable insights into the need for careful, intelligent selection of books for children.

BULLETIN BOARD IDEA

COMMENT: New book jackets should appear as often as once a week. Other identifying cards should be available with such captions as: **SCIENCE, CHRISTMAS CHEER, ADVENTURE, MISUNDERSTANDING, MEMORIES,** etc. This is a board students could plan. They will come up with much more interesting captions.

2

Providing Experiences in Creative Dramatics

Including creative dramatics in the regular school program

Participation in an assigned class assembly for the year is not enough to be considered the creative dramatics experience children should have in school. The benefits of providing continuing exploration of the dramatic arts during each school year are social, personal, and academic. Socially, a child has opportunities to (1) think out solutions of problems arising among his peers, and (2) be subjected to the healthy give and take of ideas and criticism. Personally, creative dramatics helps a child answer a deep need for understanding and controlling his environment and for trying and testing his future roles in adult society. Academically, through creative dramatics, a child puts into practice his emerging oral skills. He may also extend his understanding of the literature he has read. And if a child experiments with writing scripts he is having a practical and realistic experience with the necessary skills of written language. Drama activities may prove helpful also to the child who has reading problems, since often he needs increased self-confidence and an expanded backlog of life experiences in order to succeed with the reading act.

If creative dramatics is to be a part of the regular school program, time, space, and materials must be provided. From

15 to 30 minutes per day is desirable, though three days a week may be more suitable for some teachers. In many schools the auditorium or multi-purpose room can be scheduled for use. In most schools, children, who understand the need to be considerate of other classrooms, can make effective use of the hallway near their own rooms. Those rooms with exits to the outside have useful space for creative dramatics experiences. Finally, the classroom itself can be quite satisfactory. The space at the front or back can become the stage area, or where furniture can easily be moved the classroom can provide a theater-in-the-round setting.

Materials for creative dramatics usually should be quite simple, for the emphasis should be on effective action and dialogue, not on scenery and costumes. The most elaborate costumes and stage sets will not succeed if the dialogue is rambling and inarticulate and the action is either missing or near-chaotic. With most children the chairs, desks and tables of the classroom are sufficient for props. The very young children will find stimulation in a "dress-up" box containing castoff clothes and shoes of parents and of teenaged brothers and sisters. Occasionally, when a group of children want to put on a carefully developed production, they should use old pasteboard boxes, butcher paper, and tempera paints to create *their own* scenery. Where scenery seems necessary to the students you should encourage them to make *simple* sets that do no more than suggest the idea.

Again, I must repeat, children's creative dramatics experiences should concentrate on developing and perfecting dialogue and action, not on building scenery and begging mothers to sew detailed, authentic costumes. Yes, boys and girls are eager to plan sets and costumes, largely because they feel that providing tangible elements will compensate for their imagined inability to create action and dialogue. The best way to overcome this lack of confidence is to have frequent experiences of trying out various dramatic actions and dialogues, not to cover up with misspent energy developing props. I tell the children, "We want to be sure we have a story to tell the audience. If we can tell it well through what we do and what we say then it won't matter whether we have props or not." In fact, why waste time on props if your story to be dramatized fails to hold the interest of the audience?

Ways to get started

Since action and dialogue are paramount to successful creative dramatics, these are the areas to begin developing as soon as the school year opens. At all grade levels there can be early emphasis on activities that stimulate creative efforts to portray a variety of actions and dialogues.

Pantomime insists on appropriate actions. All school children can be encouraged to do pantomimes. I often initiate this activity by doing several pantomimes myself. When the teacher participates some reluctant students may find it easier to decide that this is something worth doing. And when you involve yourself in the development of a convincing pantomime you will better understand the efforts your students make. You will learn about the problems of communicating an action effectively. I try to select something very common, such as shoveling snow; something timely, such as a protester in a public march or a citizen voting; something from familiar literature, such as when I pantomime the baby bear who discovers Goldilocks. After I do a pantomime I re-awaken my awareness of those children who find it embarrassing to perform in front of an audience. As soon as a child identifies my pantomime correctly I suggest that he do one for the class. Whoever correctly guesses the pantomimes is next to create a new one for us. If the competition for guessing gets to be more important than the developing of effective pantomimes, then it is time to eliminate the competition aspect. The purpose of the pantomime is to convey successfully a particular action. Each child should be striving to perfect actions that communicate. If the competition element seems to be overshadowing the real purpose, then it may be wise to have each student announce beforehand what action he is going to portray.

Students are capable of creating their own pantomime actions. These need to be supported by praise and audience enthusiasm. But sometimes it is helpful to have many different children interpret the same pantomime situation. The world around us is full of possible situations which you can enjoy defining, but here is a list with which to start:

1. Someone in the kitchen preparing a dish of food by following a recipe.
2. A boy or girl in a play activity such as jumping rope, catching or batting a ball, or hiding and then running in free in the game hide-and-go-seek.
3. Threading a needle, peeling an onion, hammering a nail, pouring a pitcher of liquid.
4. Expressing feelings such as fear, happiness, disgust, anticipation.

Individual pantomimes can be followed by pairs of children creating a situation where there must be interaction between each other. These may be planned, but impromptu situations are very useful, too. Doing sketches involving a sales clerk and a customer in a variety of shops is challenging. You might tell two students, privately, to do a scene in a pet shop. Then when the sketch is completed the rest of the class should be able to decide what kind of shop it was, who the clerk was, and who the customer. Other shops you might suggest are:

1. Ice cream shop
2. Bakery
3. Toy shop
4. Florist

Pantomiming can also be done to music: marches, sea life, western themes, syncopation. Children might try different music for specific pantomimes and let the class decide which music provided the best background.

The old favorite game of charades is also a way of pantomiming. But remember the purpose for pantomiming is to develop action that is effective in communicating, so whenever a game becomes more important than the purpose, it is time to stop the game so that proper concentration can be put on the basic

purpose of doing pantomimes. You need to help children discover the pleasure of observing fine improvisation rather than
competing to be first to guess what is happening.

Development of brief dialogue also has a place at the beginning of the school year in your initial creative dramatics experiences. Begin with simple monologues using common expressions such as "come in," or "hello," and also various commands.
Ask the child to try the expression several times, once to show
anger, then to show boredom, then to show excitement or pleasure, and finally to exhibit fear. You might make tagboard signs
with each of these moods, then suggest that a student select one
card, hold it face down, give his expression, ask the class to
identify which mood was used, and then reveal the card to see
if the class was correct. If it was not, then it would be profitable
to have a discussion by the class members of the reasons for
their decision as well as an explanation by the performing student as to his choice of tone and facial movements for demonstrating a particular mood.

Another monologue activity is pretending that a visitor has
just knocked at the door. By the choice of words and tone used
by the student who is opening the door, the rest of the class
should be able to identify the imaginary visitor. A variety of
possible visitors could be written on a series of cards. A student
then volunteers to draw a card and attempt to receive the type
of visitor listed on the card. Possible visitors might include:
salesman, policeman, close friend, beggar, neighbor, and a
stranger.

Simple dialogues between two people can be developed, such
as a telephone conversation or a customer and sales person in
situations that call for decisions to be made, complaints to be
explored, and requests for such things as information, help, attendance at social functions. The main consideration in any
dialogue is to say something worth hearing, to avoid rambling
and padding. If the children know the specific purpose of the
dialogue they are engaging in, they will have a firm foundation
on which to evaluate the success of the dialogue.

Even though pantomime, monologue, and dialogue may be

considered as excellent starting points for beginning a year's program in creative dramatics, these are activities that should occur frequently throughout the year. The various holidays and other school activities will lend themselves to pantomime and development of brief dialogues. Whenever a group becomes bogged down in a more complex creative dramatics experience it may prove helpful to pause long enough to work through the problem by means of practice pantomimes or dialogues. For instance, if the action in a fairy tale seems unclear or without purpose, let several alternative possibilities be pantomimed and then evaluated by the group. The best desired action should finally be realized.

A suggested sequence

Many creative dramatics experiences should originate with the children. If time is regularly available and children are permitted to work in small groups rather than as a whole class, new and fresh ideas for dramatization will continually appear. Despite this freedom of structure it is wise to plan a flexible sequence of dramatization experiences in order that children will grow in their ability to create, solve problems, and discover new ideas. The illustrated chart suggests a plan for the year. It must be used with flexibility.

There are numerous situations you can set up for simple role playing. At Halloween several children may volunteer to be a family who lives in a house at the end of an alley (use the front of the classroom for the house and an aisle near the wall as the alley). The family characters should decide about themselves, i.e. children, adults, friendly, mean, etc. Then ask one child from the class to go up the alley and trick-or-treat at the house. When that child is finished send a pair of students, followed by another individual child, then a group of four or five. I have usually succeeded in getting every child to participate. Occasionally it helps to change the children who are portraying the family. Each person or group should be encouraged to ap-

SUGGESTED SEQUENTIAL CREATIVE DRAMATICS PROGRAM FOR THE YEAR

Activity	Place	Participants	Audience
1. Exploration of simple pantomimes and dialogues	Classroom	All students, as individuals or in pairs	Classmates
2. Simple role playing	Classroom	Small volunteer groups	Classmates
3. Creative drama initiated by students	Classroom or stage	Small volunteer groups	Invited guests or none
4. Simple stories— original or from literature	Classroom	Small volunteer groups	Classmates or none
5. More simple pantomimes or dialogues—possibly working on problems that have been observed up to this time	Classroom	All students, as individuals or in pairs	Classmates
6. More creative drama initiated by students	Classroom or stage	Small volunteer groups	Invited guests or none
7. Dramatize a story with no props— emphasis on dialogue and action	Use classroom as theater-in-the-round	Whole class	None
8. More role playing	Classroom	Small volunteer groups	Classmates
9. Dramatize a story with props but done entirely as a pantomime	Use classroom or stage	Small groups	Classmates or invited guests
10. More creative drama initiated by students	Classroom or stage	Small volunteer groups	Invited guests or none
11. Dramatize a story with props, lights, curtains, if possible	Stage or equivalent	Whole class	Invited guests

proach the house and the family in a new way, one that has not been tried yet by any of the preceding children.

Another possibility for role playing is to tell one child to imagine he is in the school hall and finds a lunch ticket on the floor. Let the child decide what to do after this. Sometimes, as I sit in the back of the room, I quietly suggest to another child that he be the principal or a fellow student and go up to interact with the first individual. When a child who has found the lunch ticket indicates he is going to the cafeteria to use the ticket, I may quickly get someone to slip up front to become the ticket-taker at the door of the imagined cafeteria.

The dramatizations suggested in the chart to be initiated by the students are usually prepared at noon, during recess, or after school. These are not evaluated unless the participants request it. And though it is important that student-initiated dramatizations be performed where other children can see them, the performers should be free to choose their own audience. Sometimes children prefer never to bring a work to a point where an audience can see it. This is not important. The most valuable learning is in the act of creating, not in finalizing the product for an audience.

Dramatizing a complete story through pantomime is an exciting challenge. Favorite fairy tales become most effective when they are pantomimed, and here students learn how necessary is appropriate action. They may wish to synchronize sound effects with pantomime action.

If you have access to an auditorium and a stage with lights and curtains your students are indeed fortunate. All students should have a real theater experience, but notice it is last in the sequence on the chart, which should keep it from becoming the major activity of your creative dramatics year. Such a complete dramatic presentation should come near the end of the year and require no more than five or six weeks at the most in preparation. Save the development of props and costumes for the very last of those six weeks. If time runs out, fine; then your students should be able to show how convincing their action and dialogue are without props.

If you do not have access to a real stage make good use of that space in the front (or rear) of the classroom. It can serve as a most adequate stage. When it is being used as such either move your desk or clear it completely. Clean the chalkboard and take down any distracting pictures, announcements, or penmanship letter cards. If you can obtain an inexpensive folding screen it would be useful in marking a place for actors to use for entrances and exits.

Are you sure it's creative?
Are you sure it's drama?

To be creative, children must be free to determine their own dialogue and actions, to establish when scenes begin and end, and to take original liberties if they are dramatizing a story from literature. Scripts are likely to prevent creative efforts, at least in the beginning, of many drama experiences. Of course, original stories are the most creative, particularly if they are developed during the actual time spent in preparing a dramatization, but tales taken from literature can also be quite creative. There should be numerous rehearsals of a story, for each time the dialogue will be altered, as will the action. Eventually, if a group of children want to perform for an audience, you may occasionally catch a clever piece of dialogue or action. When this happens to me, I say, "Try to keep that in your play. It is very effective." But truly creative performances will have new dialogue and action even on the final day when an audience is present.

The quality of drama must also be considered. Children need to learn that a dramatic situation demands an element of conflict. This conflict provides the vehicle for a drama and when the conflict is resolved the drama is at an end. Conflict can be as serious as (1) escaping from a wicked individual, (2) searching for something of value that seems to be lost, or (3) finding one's way out of a predicament. But light, humorous, or poetic drama also must have an element of conflict. It may be conflict with (1) the natural elements, (2) the moods and feelings of others, or (3) the unfulfilled wishes of someone. Early efforts of children to put on a play for an audience often fail because they really do not get anywhere; the story rambles along depicting a series of scenes in the lives of the characters but without the essential conflict factor. Time should be taken to help children in these unsuccessful efforts decide what conflicts are going to exist. Once this is clear the actor usually will be successful in resolving the problems and producing a drama.

Occasionally some children load their first efforts with too many conflicts. These children need guidance in eliminating some of the problems and developing a tighter, more cohesive dramatization. It may be that a series of conflicts are part of an overall problem, and each conflict may serve as the drama for separate scenes.

Literature as a basis for creative dramatics

The world of children's literature is filled with dramatic possibilities. Very young children will delight in Mother Goose rhymes as motivation for dramatic play. "Old Mother Hubbard and Her Dog" has enough verses to involve at least half a classroom. Different students should take turns being Mother Hubbard and the dog. Together the children may decide on the various containers Mother Hubbard will use to bring home the many items she goes out to get. The coffin would be heavy and she might need help in carrying it; the fish would be unpleasantly odorous and wrapped in plain paper and carried with disdain, a *long* distance from the nose; the wine could be in *breakable* bottles; the coat, hat, and shoes could all be worn. If the objects are imaginary, and they should be, the boys and girls will have to decide on gestures to use in order to communicate the specific items to the audience.

Another Mother Goose rhyme that is fun to dramatize is "Sing a Song of Sixpence." Again, numerous individuals should have the chance to be the king, the queen, and the maid. Of course, most of the children can be the blackbirds who emerge from the pie. Stress should be put on what you would do if you were a blackbird and had been caged in a small pie for hours. Some, naturally, will say they should sing, but others will have unexpected ideas. Each blackbird-child should express his idea in action. Other decisions the children need to make are these: what kind of king was he, why did he count his money, what manner of queen was she, did she like bread and honey, did the maid enjoy her work, was she young or old, what happened when the blackbird attacked her?

There are poems, suitable to different ages, for dramatic material. A favorite of mine is "The Elf and the Dormouse" by Oliver Herford.

> Under a toadstool
>   Crept a wee Elf,
> Out of the rain
>   To shelter himself.
>
> Under the toadstool,
>   Sound asleep,
> Sat a big Dormouse
>   All in a heap.
>
> Trembled the wee Elf
>   Frightened, and yet
> Fearing to fly away
>   Lest he got wet.
>
> To the next shelter—
>   Maybe a mile!
> Sudden the wee Elf
>   Smiled a wee smile.
>
> Tugged till the toadstool
>   Toppled in two.
> Holding it over him,
>   Gaily he flew.
>
> Soon he was safe home
>   Dry as could be.
> Soon woke the Dormouse—
>   "Good gracious me!
>
> Where is my toadstool?"
>   Loud he lamented.
> And that's how umbrellas
>   First were invented.

I have used this charming poem for dramatizing with first, second, and third graders. It is excellent for suggesting dramatic activity. I usually have about one-third to one-half of the class on their feet, either in the front or the rear of the classroom. I break the poem up into specific parts. First the children become the wee elf and show the rest of the class (the audience) how the elf might first notice that rain is beginning to fall, and then spy a shelter and finally creep in. At this point the members of the audience exchange with the actors, so that everyone gets to express himself as the wee elf. Then we try to show how the elves might discover the sleeping dormouse and what reactions the elves have.

When the elf gets his idea and begins tugging on the toad-stool, all of the actor-elves try in many unique ways to struggle, and tug, and eventually carry the toadstool off as an umbrella. Some actors treat the toadstool as very heavy, others as quite light once it has been uprooted. Some actors decide to chop the toadstool down, others dig up the soil around it.

Then it is time for the children to take the part of the dor-mouse. He must be awakened by the falling rain, discover his toadstool is gone, and then decide what to do. Some actors con-sider the dormouse lazy and they just decide to sleep in the rain. Other dormice dig imaginary holes or scurry over to an-other toadstool shelter.

This poem is useful because it permits all of the children to become involved quickly, for it is just as easy to have a roomful of elves as it is to have one. Each elf must deal with his own individual problem, so there is little or no confusion as the dramatization develops. Also, this poem suggests two conflicts, the frightening dormouse and the bothersome rain, and words such as "crept," "trembled," "smiled a wee smile," "tugged," "lamented," all of these, readily suggest ideas for each child in trying to dramatize this little story.

Older children, as well as young ones, can develop their dra-matic skills through brief lines from such poetry as Aileen Fisher's *In the Middle of the Night*.[1]

---

[1] Aileen Fisher, *In the Middle of the Night,* illustrated by Adrienne Adams (New York: Crowell, 1965).

After reading that a girl and her father discover a sleeping bumblebee, let your students try to characterize a buzzing bee who tires and curls up to sleep in a flower blossom. Later when the poem mentions wiggling worms, boys and girls will have great fun slithering and sliding. Whatever suggestions develop, remember to limit these activities to simple, usually one-at-a-time, actions. The acts of trembling, awakening, limping, lamenting, each of these can be developed if the activity does not get confused with too many diverse actions.

For example, the scene where Huck wakens Tom Sawyer at midnight can be enough for a class period devoted to communicating a certain mood to an audience. This scene requires one actor, Tom, for it begins when he hears Huck whistle outside. Tom is in his bedroom. He must check to be sure Sid, his half-brother, is sleeping, then crawl out of bed and dress silently. He must carefully raise the window, look back to be sure Sid is still sleeping, climb out the window, slide down the roof, and jump onto the ground. End of scene. Many students can volunteer to do this brief scene during a class period. In this scene each actor must convey the fear Tom has of waking Sid, and without props each actor must be as convincing as possible in opening an imaginary window and climbing over an imaginary windowsill. Perhaps the window squeaks as it is being opened, or perhaps Tom drops a shoe as he is dressing. In each instance he must show by facial features, strained or bent posture, Tom's fear of being discovered.

The vast literature of fairy tales provides fine material for dramatization. Brief moments in such tales can be used for developing dramatic skill; *for example,* the day when the stepmother awakens and goes to the mirror only to learn that Snow White has become the fairest of all. You can discuss what kind of woman has to check every morning of her life to be sure she is the most beautiful in the land. Also, discussion should bring out suggestions for ways to demonstrate how the stepmother awakens—does she yawn, stretch? Does a wealthy, selfish woman awaken differently from someone without wealth or one who is basically kind?

Another brief episode for skill development is the moment the wicked stepmother finds the dwarfs' cottage in the woods and goes up to the door in the disguise of a beggar lady. Without props it is necessary to communicate to the audience that the character begins as the haughty stepmother, searching in the woods, and then changes her character in order to deceive Snow White when she comes to the door. Each child who volunteers to do this brief scene will have ideas to contribute in developing a convincing dramatic moment.

I have found familiar fairy tales an excellent vehicle for older children to dramatize before younger audiences. Such stories as Rumpelstiltskin, Jack and the Beanstalk, Hansel and Gretel, and the Emperor's New Clothes are great fun to act out. This is a fine way for older children to have new contacts with former favorite stories, and it is also a good way to bring fairy tales alive to the very young children.

It is best to have a number of collections of fairy tales available in the room for the children to browse through. The students should usually select their own stories to dramatize. A class of 30 can divide into five groups, each one selecting a different story. Whether the stories have more or fewer characters than the number of children in the group does not matter. This is where the children can introduce their own creative modifications. Once I had a group of six do the Three Bears. They decided to give the bears a butler and a friend to join Goldilocks. Another time we were short of girls in a group doing Hansel and Gretel, so Hansel got a brother, Peter, instead.

As for the problem of deciding who will play which character, I ordinarily ask the group to practice the story several times, each time rotating the characters. Then the group is better able to select the best person for each role. Once a boy insisted on being the fisherman in The Fisherman and The Three Wishes, but after he had taken his turn as the fish and received the acclaim of his peers for his very clever interpretation, he was quite willing to change his mind.

How to evaluate progress

Evaluation in creative dramatics is an ongoing activity. Each time we dramatize something, no matter how brief, we should stop to discuss the reactions of both the audience and the players. Usually following such discussion there should be more rehearsals followed again by evaluation from the group. The teacher should remain in the audience, particularly when preparing an elaborate, complete dramatization for an invited audience. Such a performance must be the responsibility of the children from establishing dialogues and actions to managing lights and curtains. If the teacher is always in the audience, even for evaluative comments, the children will realize the responsibility they have and assume it. I remember from my own childhood that my sixth-grade teacher talked a great deal about the fact that on the day of the performance we would be on our own. But every day of practice she was on stage directing students, making decisions about curtains and lights. On the day of performance she joined the audience and we fell apart. If you expect children to handle themselves independently, you must allow them to do so *from the beginning*.

I make it a practice to have the cast come out and sit on stage after each rehearsal while I, sitting in the audience, make my suggestions. I do not go on stage to explain what I am saying. In effect, I make the stage the children's responsibility. Here are the two major comments I give whenever I am evaluating a group: (1) Communicate with your audience. Be sure your audience knows what is going on, what is said, and why. (2) Lose yourself in the character you are playing. From the moment you go before the audience you are no longer Johnny or Mary or a third grader or a fifth grader; you are the wicked witch, the mighty giant, a clever Hansel, etc. You will be as successful as the degree to which you lose yourself and become the character. I often mention favorite television characters and explain how surprised we would be to see these people when they are not acting, for these professionals seem perfect in losing themselves and developing a character that is so convincing we believe the character to be the real person.

There is also the need to comment on speaking so the audience can hear and doing important action where the audience can see. These comments may have to be made by you, but they are more meaningful when classmates who have served as audience can be involved in evaluation sessions.

Suggested audiences

The most common audience should be the other children from your class. As audience members they will be quite helpful in suggesting changes and improvements. Classmates as audience help to bind the class into an effective learning group.

At times other audiences are desirable. Children who have worked long and seriously on a dramatization want to share their efforts with others. Generally the acting group should determine the audience. It may be the room next door. It may be classes of a different grade level. It may be the whole school. It is also possible that a self-initiated dramatization by a group of girls would be best for an audience made up only of girls. The same is true for a boys' dramatization and a male audience. Occasionally a final, carefully developed performance is one to which the group wishes to invite parents or children from a neighboring school. But the performing group should make the decision about who will constitute the audience.

It is possible that a group may finally decide that no audience should see the play. It may never have reached a point where the children are satisfied. This does not mean the time spent on practice and evaluation has been wasted. You and I may never know the valuable learnings that have come from this time spent in creating a story, a mood, and in solving many real problems.

IN SUMMARY

1. Creative dramatics must be part of the regular curriculum.
2. Scenery and costumes are of negligible importance in comparison

to the attention that should be given to developing convincing dialogue and appropriate action.

3. Pantomimes and various simple dialogues are useful for starting a year's program of creative dramatics.
4. Most creative dramatic experiences should be the result of children's ideas, not just the teacher's ideas.
5. Our literary heritage provides material for dramatization. Even though dramas may be based on familiar stories, they should bear the mark of original interpretation.
6. Evaluation should be ongoing and involve both teacher and students.

Bibliography

SIKS, GERALDINE BRAIN, *Creative Dramatics*. New York: Harper and Row, 1958. A book to encourage the creative imagination of the child through specific guidelines and suggestions for dramatics.

————, *Children's Literature for Dramatization: An Anthology*. New York: Harper and Row, 1964. Poems and stories suitable for dramatization with brief but helpful suggestions.

SIKS, GERALDINE, and HAZEL DUNNINGTON, editors. *Children's Theater and Creative Dramatics*. Seattle: University of Washington Press, 1961. Leaders in this field have contributed articles on the philosophy, history, principles, and practices of both children's theater and creative drama.

WARD, WINIFRED, *Playmaking with Children* (2nd ed.). New York: Appleton-Century-Crofts, Inc., 1957. A standard reference for this field including consideration of therapy and speech improvement in playmaking.

Photographs of children in natural classroom poses

Photographs of the same children displaying appropriate facial and other body reactions for specific characters in a dramatization

BULLETIN BOARD IDEA

COMMENT: A polaroid camera would be quite handy to catch students IN CHARACTER during play rehearsals. Avoid using pictures of children in costume. This will tend to put more emphasis on costuming than you should. Put the emphasis on apparent action.

3

Involving Students in Classroom Discussions

Motivating initial interest: determining what to discuss

Our lives are punctuated with social conversations; therefore, as teachers, we have a responsibility to guide students into satisfying conversations. The best way to attain ease in real life social conversation is to have frequent practice in school. Much of anyone's conversation is of a rambling nature, touching on a series of unrelated subjects, but a directed conversation, or discussion, has a set subject. Such vocal interchange requires careful thought based upon some background of experience gained through reading and personal participation. The subject of a discussion is usually one that insists on a resolution of some problem or a decision for some course of action. It may also serve to clarify or edify.

I fear that much of what we teachers identify as discussion in our classes is little more than a series of one-to-one exchanges between individual students and the teacher. It is a temptation to think a discussion is taking place when one's lesson plan for the day reads, "Discuss what we've learned to date in social studies," when, in truth, what actually does happen is that the teacher has a set of questions designed to elicit facts, not discussion, and each student in the class plays a game of listen-till-you're-off-the-hook. This is the game where a student listens until someone is called on, then the student can relax, and the one who was called on, if he does not know the answer, ceases to listen when the teacher goes to another person to answer the question. Students have us well figured out. We seldom call on the same child in close succession. We usually call for facts, not expansion of ideas. We initiate the talking, not the children, so it becomes unnecessary for one child to hear what another child is saying.

Real discussion cannot operate this way. Instead, it must resemble a basketball game. The ball is the idea being tossed around. It may be the teacher who throws it out, at first, but the teacher is either one of the players or the referee, depending upon the ability of the group to conduct its own discussion. Once the ball is in the game it is moved about from player to player until finally a point is made. The important thing is that the ball may go back and forth among several players a number of times, and the rest of the team remains alert for the time when it can take the ball and advance it. The same should happen to an idea in a discussion. First, it must be an idea, not just a fact, and the idea must travel back and forth, without teacher intervention, between students, and the students must remain alert to grab on to the idea and help to develop it by the addition of new points.

Example of a "dead" discussion:

TEACHER: John, where is Lake Michigan located?
JOHN: (*Silence, eyes down, more silence*)
TEACHER: Yes, Mary you tell us.

And where is your attention? On Mary. How about John? He has breathed a sigh of relief, and his attention is *not* on Mary; why should it be? The teacher is through with him. Only an unkind, sarcastic person would later jump back and say, "Now, John, where is Lake Michigan located?" And when he still did not know, such a teacher would say, "I thought you weren't listening. If you would pay attention you would learn." This is not professional. John can expect most of his teachers to be professional. And so he can also depend on his teachers to leave him alone once he has recited in a class "discussion."

Example of a "live" discussion:

TEACHER: How does the location of Lake Michigan influence our lives?

JOHN: (*volunteering to speak*) Well, it's one of the Great Lakes. (*long pause*)

TEACHER: Can anyone explain how the information John has given us contributes to the effect of Lake Michigan on us by its location?

MARY: Well, it's the southernmost of the Great Lakes, so you might say most of the Great Lakes empty into Lake Michigan.

JOHN: And the Great Lakes are connected to the Atlantic Ocean by the St. Lawrence Seaway, so that means Lake Michigan is really connected to the ocean.

BOB: But I don't see how that affects us.

MARY: Well, Chicago is the major port on Lake Michigan.

JOHN: And we depend on Chicago for much of our needs.

BOB: So, Chicago is really connected to the Atlantic Ocean.

As a teacher you must plan carefully for a real basketball game discussion. The questions you phrase need to make students think, not just repeat memorized facts, but rather to *use* facts in contributing to the construction of ideas. When students realize that they can take what others say and build upon it, they will cease to "turn-off" when a teacher is talking to someone else. Hopefully, the teacher will not be talking so much now, and the students will feel a commitment to involvement in class discussion.

TRADITIONAL MAP OF CLASS-
ROOM INTERCHANGE

MORE DESIRABLE MAP OF
CLASSROOM INTERCHANGE

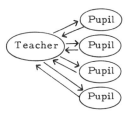
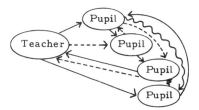

The subject matter of discussions is as broad as the curriculum and as specific as present student concerns. Discussions cannot be assigned from a list of topics in an English textbook, nor can there be a unit on discussion unless it comes early in the year and you, as teacher, use it as a starting place knowing that discussions must occur throughout the school year. Discussion is a basic means of communication and thereby of learning. So it cannot be treated within the confines of a unit. Discussion goes on daily. Its success will depend on your ability to phrase questions, to field ideas from one speaker to another, and to refrain from imposing your beliefs upon the group.

Discussions should occur in social studies, reading, science, and mathematics classes. Here are sample questions that may lend themselves to discussion: (As teacher you will have to avoid the temptation to tell, to lecture, to indoctrinate.)

Social Studies

1. Would ___(name of place)___ be a wise location for a ___(type, i.e. apple juice, frozen vegetable, clothing)___ industry?
2. Could our community get along without ___(Name of service organization, i.e. police, doctors, etc.)___?

Reading

1. Do you think ___(name of character)___ in the story is speaking for the author?
2. How might ___(name of character)___ act in another situation?

Science

1. Make predictions concerning materials to be combined.
2. Answer the question "why" following an experiment.

Mathematics

1. How many different ways can we ___(multiply, divide, subtract)___ ? Is one way better than another?
2. Why learn math when there are computers to do the work for us?

There are many discussion topics that arise from student concerns. It may be that the time set aside for language arts is the best time for a discussion of these topics, but on the other hand a concern that needs attention in an elementary classroom should get it immediately. You would therefore be justified in calling such a discussion, whenever it occurs, part of your language arts, for the way to learn *how* to have a discussion is to *have* a discussion. Such concerns as the following may occur and thus become subjects to talk about:

1. Disagreements that arise on the playground.
2. Social conflict such as a clique that attempts to control others.
3. Problems that arise in the lunchroom (messy tables, lack of respect for the cook), in the library (conflict of interests affecting use of the library), in the classroom (too much noise, inequitable availability of facilities).
4. Current issues that arouse interest of the students such as local decisions of the city council that affect the parks and streets; statewide problems such as air and water pollution, need for recreational areas, etc.; national and international crises involving race, war, fashions, and resistance to the establishment.

All of the preceding are subjects that can result in numerous stimulating, thought-provoking discussions, but they seldom can be successfully planned ahead of time by the teacher. The teacher must be ready for the critical moment when children bring up a subject. This will only happen in an environment where children feel free to express themselves and are encouraged to think together. Such an environment comes into being when there is a teacher who is a good listener, who has ideas of his own but honestly and sincerely accepts the ideas of others.

Children learn to be their own discussion leaders

At every age boys and girls should frequently have the experience of leading a group discussion. This is the best possible way to learn about discussions. In the very early grades it is unlikely that children would be designated as discussion leaders, but there should be times when individual children are asked by the teacher to sit down with two or three or four others to talk about a subject *of interest to them.* After a short time has been allowed for these simple discussions, the teacher should pull the class together to talk about what has taken place in the small groups. By such comments as, "Did everyone get to say the things he wanted?" "Was it hard to wait and let someone else talk?" "What did someone say that made you think?" the teacher begins to establish some basic ideas about discussions. Very young children can become aware of the need to allow everyone a chance to express himself, and begin to accept the idea that one should think about and react to what others say.

As children enter third and fourth grades, discussions can last longer with individual children serving as leaders. At times students can volunteer to be leaders, at other times they can be selected by the class, and occasionally the teacher may choose the leaders. As designated leaders these children will face the same problems of the younger children: (1) giving everyone an equal chance to be heard, and (2) building ideas out of what has been said. Again, teachers need to engage the class in discussions *about* the discussions, and in this way students will learn what contributes to more successful discussions. Rules set down in a textbook will have little meaning.

Children in fifth and sixth grades should not only have their own discussion leaders but they should also evaluate the success of different leaders. These older students can continue to have discussions in small groups of five to ten, but sometimes the leaders should have the experience of conducting a discussion involving the entire class.

An experiment in student-directed discussion

We owe our children guidance in helping them develop self-direction. This includes carrying on discussions without the teacher. Students must have opportunities for decision-making and then experiencing the consequences of their decisions. I heard a pediatrician tell a parent-teacher group, "We should be training our children to be independent from the day they are born. Independence isn't something that just happens at 16 or

21." In fact, the child who has been denied a chance to be self-directed will enter the adult world with the handicap of dependency.

Each day you must ask yourself, "What did I do to encourage independent thought and action on the part of my students?" From allowing a responsible kindergarten child to use a pair of pointed scissors, to providing primary and middle grade children a choice of materials for a variety of activities, to encouraging fifth- and sixth-grade students to plan their whole day's course of action—all of these have great potential in demonstrating to children the responsibility and challenge of self-direction.

The following is a description of an experiment I had with a mixed group of fourth, fifth, and sixth graders learning to cope with a student-directed discussion. It may suggest ideas for you to try in your classroom. It surely will point up some notable factors necessary for discussion, for self-direction, and for the teacher's role in student self-directed discussions.

I began one day by setting before the class a problem the librarian was having which involved an unnecessary amount of time spent on her part in sending out overdue notices. I said this was taking the librarian away from the more important work of helping students in the library locate needed materials, and it was also keeping such material out of circulation. Then I asked the class to speculate on what would happen if I were to leave the room at this time, to return at the end of the period for a report of their decisions which I then could deliver to the librarian. The reaction of most children was that chaos would occur. As one child put it, "We'd just goof off if you left." So I used the remainder of this class period leading a discussion as to why so many children felt the teacher's presence was necessary to avoid "goofing off." When I asked, "Do you really believe the only way to have order in a classroom is to have the teacher here enforcing it?" many children agreed. One said, "Oh, a few would try to discuss the problem, but most everyone would fool around, and it would be hard to accomplish anything." I pressed for reasons why the students would become distracted and lose order in the teacher's absence. Their answers were most interesting, including two fundamental thoughts: (1) there needs to be a leader, and (2) everyone is not interested in the subject being discussed.

I chose to pursue the idea of having a leader. This was an attractive idea and soon we held an election. After the leader was chosen I told the class I would leave for the remainder of the period and that on the next day we would attempt to discuss two items: (1) the success of the leader, and (2) the decisions made concerning the subject under discussion. Of course, we did not get beyond the first item. When the class began the next day, Charlie, the elected leader, began by saying, "I was a flop. We had a mess." Trying to discover the causes for the leader's evident failure became the topic for the day's discussion. The result was a realization that the elected leader, Charlie, was in fact a minority winner. Charlie was one of five candidates the class had nominated. This was a class of 18 and here was the vote:

Charlie	6	Butch	2
Greg	5	Nina	1
Molly	4		

It had appeared to the class that Charlie was the winner, but now the students realized he did not have the support of even half of the class. The group decided to eliminate the two lowest vote-recipients, then vote again, planning to eliminate the lowest again if someone did not receive ten votes, a true majority. The fact that a majority really means one more than half had never occurred to the students, but when so many children found it impossible to accept Charlie's leadership they soon discovered that most of them, a majority, had not voted for him in the first place.

After Greg was elected by the class, I again set up the next class period to be conducted in my absence. On the following day I met with the students and we discussed how things had gone. There was a general feeling that the discussion had achieved considerable success. The students were beginning to understand that if the leader's success depended on them, since

in truth they had chosen him, then it mattered whether he succeeded or not. His failure would be a reflection on their poor
judgment, and so they made a fine effort to support their leader.

Despite this understanding by the group, on the next day
when I again removed myself from the class the problems of
control arose, and when I returned to discuss their latest independent session, Greg was distressed for he felt he was failing.
We then began to look at the role of a leader. Greg had assumed
that once he was elected he was the boss. It was not long before
the class resented his unilateral decisions for maintaining order
and began to rebel. I pointed out that since leaders are elected
into office they can also be voted out as well. An elected official
is a representative of a group and must, therefore, find out the
will of the group. After these problems of discipline were
brought before the class, decisions were made collectively regarding "punishment." Again, the leader experienced considerable success because he was enforcing rules the group had
determined.

These student-directed discussions continued with new leaders
chosen periodically, with topics of genuine interest being discussed, and eventually with me, the teacher, present at all times
but as a *participant,* not as the "power behind the throne."

Procedures for evaluation

The experience I have just described of a student-directed discussion was carefully tied together through an ongoing evaluation. My general procedure was to follow each day when I had
absented myself with a day in which I conducted a discussion
about how the period without me had gone. In effect, I was
conducting an evaluation session on alternating days, using the
discussion procedure. The most effective way to evaluate progress in carrying on discussions is through discussion itself.

What do you talk about in these evaluative discussions? I
have already mentioned the problem of so-called majority decisions, the function of an elected leader, and the responsibility
of the group members to keep the leader aware of the repre-

sentation they expect. In addition, time should be taken to discuss each individual's reactions. Did you get to contribute ideas to the group? If not, why not? Did you desire to contribute? For what reasons? What about problems of individuals who tend to monopolize the discussion? (Someone usually says that this is a problem the leader must handle. Here is another discussion topic.)

It is possibly useful for each student in a discussion to fill out a brief evaluation form in three parts, each one being deposited in an appropriate folder for future reference as students strive to gain in their skill of carrying on discussion.

A suggested form for evaluation:

I. *The leader*   YES   NO

   1. Did he represent the majority?   ____ ____

   2. Did he represent you at any time?   ____ ____

   3. Did he see that everyone who wished had
      an equal chance to speak?   ____ ____

   4. Did he make an effort to get those who
      usually say little or nothing to contribute
      to the discussion?   ____ ____

   5. Was he successful in getting those in #4
      to speak?   ____ ____

   6. Other comments: _____

_____

II. *The group*

   1. Comment on the successes the group had in holding this
      discussion. _____

_____

_____

   2. Comment on any problems the group had in the discussion.

_____

_____

_____

III. *Yourself, as a participant in the discussion group*

   1. Did you volunteer contributions? _____

2. Do you prefer to listen and not speak during a discussion? _____

3. Was it easy to keep your thinking on the subject that was being discussed? _____

4. Other comments: _____

_____

_____

Another procedure for evaluation would be to listen to selected portions of a tape recording of a class discussion. You may be inclined to set up your own evaluation discussion and thus determine the parts of a recording to be heard, but there is great value in having a small group of two or three students plan such an evaluation session. Considerable learning may take place just in the process of listening to a recording and selecting certain parts for the class to discuss.

If possible, students should hear other discussions as a means of evaluating and learning about successful techniques. A visit to a local city council could be quite an education. Children would learn that the best rules are not always adhered to, and they should later be able to discuss the possible problems or understandable reasons for an "unorthodox" discussion. A visit to a high school meeting of the student government could provide material for your students to discuss. If your principal is willing, you might even have your class attend a faculty meeting. You might also ask the students who are in 4-H, Campfire Girls, Boy and Girl Scouts, or any other outside organization to tape record a business meeting for the class to hear.

Planning for future discussions

In general discussions should be spontaneous, arising out of problems or questions that genuinely concern your children. But it is possible also to plan some discussions related to work in social studies and science as well as discussions about books that students have read and feel strongly about.

There are many more opportunities for small group discussions than for whole-class ones. These small groups almost always are student-directed. They may be for the purpose of developing a creative dramatics performance, presenting a science demonstration, planning a class party, preparing a literature program for a primary class, discussing plans for hall or classroom bulletin boards, or introducing a film to the rest of the class for a social studies unit. The opportunities for discussions are endless. Your position as the year moves along should be less and less that of the leader and more and more that of a guide in evaluation.

IN SUMMARY

1. True discussion involves exchange and expansion of ideas, not domination by the leader and submissive responsiveness of the members of the group.
2. Subject matter for discussions arises from current concerns of the group.
3. Most students should have the experience of serving as a discussion leader.
4. Students must become increasingly adept at directing their own discussions.
5. Evaluation of discussion is best done through discussion.

Bibliography

Floyd, William Downing, "An Analysis of the Oral Questioning Activity in Selected Colorado Primary Classrooms." Unpublished doctoral dissertation, Colorado State College, Greeley, 1961. A most revealing study of the amount of teacher domination of the oral work in a classroom. It makes a strong case for the need to get children to do more of the talking.

Amidon, Edmund J., and Ned A. Flanders, *The Role of the Teacher in the Classroom*. A manual for understanding and improving teachers' classroom behavior.

Sanders, Norris M., *Classroom Questions: What Kinds?* New York: Harper and Row, 1966. An excellent guide in helping teachers construct questions that will result in more productive responses.

NOT THIS...

BUT THIS

COMMENT: Bulletin boards on current events from the international, national, local and school scenes should stimulate topic material for discussions. The unfortunate fact about many current events bulletin boards is that they soon appear cluttered and uncared for. Such boards should truly be current. They need to be attractively arranged. Clippings and pictures from newspapers and magazines should be cut neatly and often mounted. The board should attract attention, and it should change often enough so that the students are always checking on what is new.

Dialects—an Approach to the Way We Talk

Three aspects: vocabulary, pronunciation, and usage

Classroom attention to dialects is quite new, though the professional literature is beginning to address itself to this subject and to suggest implications for teaching. Since dialectology is just now reaching the elementary classroom this chapter must necessarily be brief, but it is hoped that you will be stimulated to experiment with the study of dialects, to read further in the field, and to remain alert to future publications in the professional literature which deal with incorporating the study of dialects into the elementary classroom.

Dialect is a word we usually ascribe to the speech of others outside our group. It is something we do not believe exists in our own speech. But, in fact, dialect is a pattern of speech which is used and understood by a group of people; thus all groups have their own particular dialects. Each dialect will differ in certain features: vocabulary, pronunciation, and usage (or grammar, if you prefer, but including both word construction and syntax).

Vocabulary differences of various groups are more definite than many of us realize. As teachers we have a great assortment of words peculiar to our profession: *motivation, objectives, individual differences, parent-teacher conferences, report cards,* etc. Each profession and occupation claims a particular set of words. Even hobbies and vocations have special vocabularies: a tennis player uses a *racket* and a *net;* the piano player must know about *chords, harmonies, time signatures;* the painter works in *oils* from a *palette* on a *canvas;* and the stamp collector is a *philatelist* engrossed in collecting *first-day covers, blocks,* and *commemoratives.* Vocabularies differ geographically: for example, a skillet in one part of the country is a frying pan in another, a binder here is a rubber band there, a package here is a paper sack there. Even sex differences influence vocabulary: girls wear jeans, boys wear levis, girls go to the beauty shop, boys go to the barber.

Most of us are quick to notice pronunciation differences. You say roof to rhyme with woof but I say roof to rhyme with goof. Someone says route as though it was a rhyming partner of out while others say it so that it rhymes with loot.

Usage differences are quite interesting. My wife's relatives say, "Close the light," and I say, "Turn the light off," and yet others say, "Shut the light." When a train has passed by, the Pennsylvania Dutch say, "And the little red house makes all," but I say, "There's the caboose."

Is the way you talk bad?

As a child in elementary school I remember some of my teachers ridiculing my classmates, who were first-generation Americans with parents from middle Europe, when they spoke. We have come a long way from the rather narrow view that there is only one right way to talk. We now recognize there are many influences on our speech: physical geography; degree of proximity to great cultural centers; the social class structure in which we have been raised; the effect of various immigrant groups who have come to America and given us words now common to us such as *pretzel, hamburger, pizza, chop suey;* and finally the effect of television, which must be considered as a modifying force on our spoken language. But in no way can the speech we use be classed as good or bad. Rather, it must be considered for its appropriateness in any given setting. For example, if a Hawaiian youngster spoke "pidgin English" in school he would be in trouble, but if he spoke general or standard English to his buddies in the neighborhood, he would be equally in trouble. Another example: if the coach in the heat of the ball game began talking to his team in precise, formal English, he might very well lose the game because of his failure to communicate with the boys.

For a final example: a young person, applying for a summer job where he might be expected to deal with the adult public, would have no success if he carried on his part of the interview in the current "hip" slang. Yet at the Friday night beach party he had better have command of that delightfully different and very informal language.

To say that any particular mode of speaking is incorrect, or bad, is unfair. We all speak in a variety of modes and one is not better than the other. Each one fits a particular place and audience.

Our language is losing its richness

Television probably has become the greatest equalizer of our language. From the lost folds of the Appalachians across the broad, lonely tableland of Kansas up to the isolated hamlets high in the Cascades, most of America is getting a daily dose of television English. The newscasters, the quiz show hosts, and most of the entertainers speak with amazing similarity with regard to vocabulary, pronunciation, and usage.

John Steinbeck, in his *Travels with Charley in Search of America*,[1] tells of a recent journey across America, and in describing one of his reasons for the trip he expresses his great concern for the change that is occurring in our language.

---

[1] John Steinbeck, *Travels with Charley in Search of America* (New York: Viking Press, 1962).

One of my purposes was to listen, to hear speech, accent, speech rhythms, overtones and emphasis. For speech is so much more than words and sentences. I did listen everywhere. It seemed to me that regional speech is in the process of *disappearing,* not gone but going. Forty years of radio and twenty years of television must have this impact. Communications must destroy localness, by a slow, inevitable process. I can remember a time when I could almost pinpoint a man's place of origin by his speech. That is growing more difficult now and will in some foreseeable future become impossible. It is a rare house or building that is not rigged with spiky combers of the air. Radio and television speech becomes standardized, perhaps better English than we have ever used. Just as our bread, mixed and baked, packaged and sold without benefit of accident or human frailty, is uniformly good and uniformly tasteless, so will our speech become one speech.

Ways to become familiar with dialects

Your students can become amateur field workers in dialectology. To begin their study they should learn about their own dialect differences. In class discussion lists can be made of word variants of nouns, verbs, adjectives, adverbs, and prepositions. The longest list will likely be variants of nouns. You might divide the section on nouns into the following categories: (1) food and drink, (2) artifacts, or things, (3) phenomena of nature. For example, "apple cobbler" may be known by such names as *deep-dish apple pie, apple grunt,* and *apple Jonathan.* "Chest of drawers" may be called *dresser, bureau,* or *chiffonier;* and "earthworm" may be *angleworm, bait,* or *ground worm.*

Here are a few samples of word variants for categories other than nouns:

Verb

(He is) WASTING TIME: loafing on the job, puttering around, dawdling, killing time.

Adjective

(He is quite) SKILLFUL (at some task): a hand at, clever, handy.

Adverb

(It's) RATHER (cold): kind of, sort of, middling.

Preposition

(Quarter) OF (eleven): to, till.

As the class brings out the different words used to mean similar ideas, it is necessary to recognize the fact that certain situations call for differences in one's speech. A child may explain that he uses "groovy" or "neat" or some similar expression when something pleases him as he is talking to his classmates on the school bus, but at home or in church he is more likely to say something like "very nice" or "lovely."

The boys may be willing to list words they use among each other which are different from words they use when talking about the same subject in the presence of girls. This may lead into lists of words that are related to subjects usually only of interest to boys or to girls as well as various words for the same general idea: i.e. girls may call an outer garment a "wrap" whereas boys would be quite unlikely to use that term but would identify the garment as a "sweater" or "coat"; girls get together to "gossip" and boys get together to "shoot the bull."

As students become more aware of the many differences of vocabulary among themselves, they will be ready and willing to investigate differences in pronunciation as well. There should be no stigma attached to any pronunciation. Some may say "warsh" when others say "wash." Some may say "greazy" when others say "greasy." Trying to use written symbols to express certain sounds could prove rather difficult for children; a collection of variant pronunciations recorded on tape would prove more useful.

Soon after the class members have entered into the collecting and listing of various aspects of their language they can broaden their fieldwork by attempting to map the cultural and geographical background of each student. Use outline maps of the United States and of the world to plot where relatives and ancestors came from. Efforts can be made to match vocabulary and pronunciation similarities with specific geographical and cultural origins.

As fieldworkers learning about dialects, the class should take time to listen to the speech of others. In pairs students can go to other classrooms to observe, listen, and record spoken language. A visiting pair should have some plan: for instance, one time could be concerned with variant noun usage, and another visit might concentrate on variant pronunciations, perhaps of a prescribed list developed by your class as it discovered its own variations.

The television and movies will provide another source for your amateur fieldworkers in their recording of variants in the spoken language. Visitors to the school will provide another source of study. Some child could be designated to interview a visitor to determine his geographical and cultural background. If others have listened carefully to the visitor they may have an interesting list of language variations, and these can be compared with the visitor's background and with others who might have a similar background.

The community offers an excellent resource for fieldworkers in dialect. Your students can make up lists of common nouns, verbs, and adjectives and go out into different neighborhoods and ask people to respond with the terms they use. Then the student fieldworkers should learn where the people they are interviewing come from, or where their families originated.

Some children's literature contains excellent examples of regional dialects. These will be of interest both for the varieties in vocabulary and for observing the efforts of the writer to record symbols to represent specific sounds for variant pronunciations.

In Ester Wier's *The Barrel* [2] the following passage is indica-

---

[2] Ester Wier, *The Barrel* (New York: McKay, 1966).

tive of the Florida swamp dialect contained in this excellent story:

> "Wasn't skeert at all," Turpem was boasting. "My brother and his dog, both of 'em, faced right up to that hog. Chance wouldn't git up in the tree without he took Angus with him, and that leetle dog give the tusker a real whirl-a-round. Kept sashayin' this way and that and fussed him up real good. Never saw anythin' like how brave the two of 'em was."

You and the children can become alert to various efforts at reproducing dialects in the different books chosen for recreational reading. It might prove most interesting to compare how several authors treat the same type of dialect; for instance, Marguerite De Angeli in *Yonie Wondernose* [3] and Lois Lenski in *Shoo-Fly Girl* [4] both tell stories of Amish families, but the use of dialect is somewhat different.

Your students might choose to make a special project of their dialect fieldwork resulting in a report. The subject of a report might be one block in the neighborhood, or of a student's own family. Such a report should include word lists and notes on pronunciation variations. It could contain outline maps where the backgrounds of the informants are plotted.

Older children might make a study of the origin of words. They could try to discover why "tidy up," "clean up," and "redd up" all came into use for the same general idea. This could be done with any of the variant forms the student fieldworkers discovered. A variety of dictionaries would need to be available, not just the usual simplified ones that abound in elementary schools.

Another activity the students can engage in is playing a mystery game. Differences in the vocabulary of an individual can tell others a lot about that person. Certain words will indicate how old we are; i.e. someone who says "ice box" is much

---

[3] Marguerite - DeAngeli, *Yonie Wondernose* (New York: Doubleday Doran, 1944).

[4] Lois Lenski, *Shoo-Fly Girl* (Philadelphia: Lippincott, 1963).

older than someone who says "refrij." Our vocabulary may also identify whether we are male or female; i.e. a girl may say something looks "cute" or "divine," but a boy is more likely to say it looks "great" or "swell." A person also reveals his educational background through his choice of words. The specialized vocabulary of occupational groups identifies one's line of work. And finally, some words indicate our origins.

Students might collect samples of conversation on a tape recorder, then play them back to the class to attempt an identification of age, education, occupation, and origin of the speakers. Transcriptions of conversations could be used to solve the mystery of whether a speaker is male or female. Some students may wish to try their skill in creating, either written or spoken, a sample of language suitable to a specific age, sex, education, occupation, and/or origin and then request the class to determine the individual who might have spoken this sample.

Other students will find it a challenge to locate a variety of speech communities close at hand, perhaps no farther away than the school. Some speech communities would be the office, the classroom, the play field, and the kitchen. Outside of school the children might study the speech communities of different business offices, occupational groups, clubs, and service organizations such as the fire station, hospital, and telephone company. Your students will suggest many more speech communities for study.

A final experience your students might explore is learning to speak a different dialect. Discovering examples in their library reading as well as listening to specific dialects on television will provide a source of material to learn. Comedian routines on television often utilize easily identifiable dialects. The students might begin by trying to imitate what they hear or read. Then they could attempt original conversation in the same dialect.

It is important to remember in any of these activities that one's interest in other people's dialects is for the purpose of becoming more aware of one's own dialect, not to ridicule or demean others. It also helps us to savor and maintain the rich beauty of our language in its variant forms.

IN SUMMARY

1. Dialect is a part of everyone's speech, distinguished by vocabulary, pronunciation, and usage.
2. General English may be desirable in many settings, but other dialects are essential in specific situations, so it is not our task to eliminate variant dialects, but to guide students toward an understanding and acceptance of the usefulness of general English.
3. Becoming an amateur fieldworker in dialectology is a valuable experience for students in developing a growing love of language.
4. As dialect fieldworkers we can tap a most productive resource, the community.
5. A growing love for language includes developing respect for the many possible dialect varieties and striving to keep a rich, vivid quality to our language.

Bibliography

MALMSTROM, JEAN, and ANNABEL ASHLEY, *Dialects: U.S.A.* National Council of Teachers of English, 1963. A concise statement defining dialects and attempting to suggest causes. It discusses dialect distribution throughout the country. A bibliography is included for those who wish to become better acquainted with this field.

SHUY, ROGER W., *Discovering American Dialects.* National Council of Teachers of English, 1967. Much of this brief book is devoted to the dialect fieldworker and how he goes about his fascinating task.

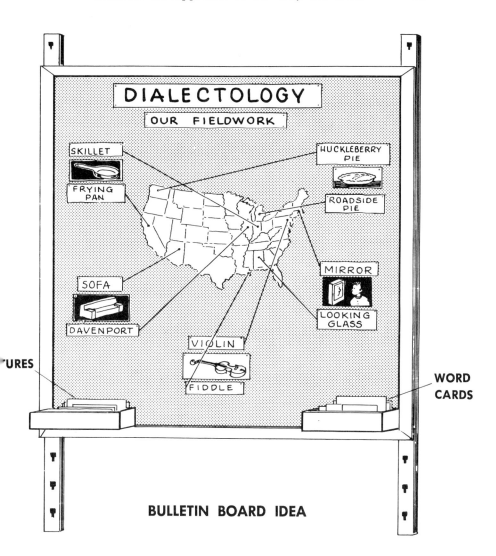

BULLETIN BOARD IDEA

COMMENT: Beneath the bulletin board place a container of pictures and another of words. For example, the words SKILLET and FRYING PAN should be located for the areas of common usage on the map, and then identified with the appropriate picture.

5

Developing Effective Oral Talks

Let's begin with sharing time

Oral talks probably begin with the youngest child who comes to school and has something to tell his teacher. This becomes the popular sharing time, or show-and-tell-time. It is natural for children to want to tell someone about their experiences—and how fortunate boys and girls are who find at school a time and place to tell others about what has happened to them. The child, beginning in kindergarten, needs to be permitted, and, in some cases, encouraged to share experiences. For the very young this sharing time should occur each day, preferably at the beginning of the morning since many children enter the classroom eager to show or tell something they have stored up in their minds since awakening or even something they planned as they fell asleep the night before.

Effective sharing demands appropriate teacher reactions

A time for sharing should be carefully thought out by the teacher. It is not a time for taking lunch count or checking papers. You need to hear what each child has to say, for you must react to each child's oral contribution. Such reaction is not necessarily an oral comment during the sharing time. It may be a facial expression or, later, a reference to the child's sharing when you are engaging a group of children in conversation. It may be identifying books, pictures from your file, or objects in your personal collection that relate to the subject of a child's sharing. Of course, you often will make comments immediately after a child finishes his sharing. Such comments must have genuine meaning, and must not be glibly spoken or based on a vague hearing of what the child said. Often your comments should serve to extend the child's interest in continued inquiry into various subjects. Sharing time is a time when concept development is taking place. Frequently, as a sharing period draws to a close, you should ask yourself: what concepts were given attention today? A simple record might be kept for primary children as in Figure 5-1.

SHARING TIME RECORD

Name _____

Date _____

Subject shared _____

Main concepts given attention _____

_____

Other comments _____

_____

Figure 5-1

A collection of such slips in a child's folder would permit you to periodically assess his growth in certain concepts as well as his variety, or lack of it, of subjects shared. This suggested form is so brief it would only take moments to complete, yet it could prove a useful data source for evaluating a child's progress.

Here is an example of the way a teacher might contribute to concept development of the children:

CHILD: I saw some pretty flowers on the way to school.

TEACHER: This is the time of year when flowers are beginning to bloom.

ANOTHER CHILD: We don't have any flowers in our yard.

TEACHER: You may have some flowers that haven't bloomed yet. Each day you should check your yard to see if any flowers have bloomed.

A THIRD CHILD: Teacher, I brought you some flowers.

TEACHER: Oh, thank you. Aren't they pretty? Oh, look, here is one that is still a bud. It hasn't bloomed yet. Let's put these blooming flowers and this bud in some water, then we can watch the bud bloom.

Here the teacher has carefully used the word *bloom* in context and by thoughtful repetition she is helping the children develop a fuller concept of the blooming of flowers. This conversation might have gone another direction if other comments had been made by the children, for example:

CHILD: I saw some pretty flowers on the way to school.

TEACHER: This is the time of year when flowers are beginning to bloom.

ANOTHER CHILD: It used to be cold when I got up in the morning. Now it's warmer.

TEACHER: This time of year, when things are getting warmer, is called spring.

THIRD CHILD: What comes after spring?

TEACHER: Summer. That is when it is very warm, even hot.

And so begins a conversation in which the concept of the spring season may become firmly established in the minds of the children. Here is yet a third direction the conversation might have taken:

CHILD: I saw some pretty flowers on the way to school.

TEACHER: This is the time of year when flowers are beginning to bloom.

SAME CHILD: So I picked some for you. They all look alike.

TEACHER: Oh, thank you. Aren't they pretty? They do look alike. Can someone tell us one way they look alike?

ANOTHER CHILD: They are all red.

THIRD CHILD: They all have long black things inside.

FOURTH CHILD: They look like fancy dishes.

TEACHER: You are all using good eyes. These flowers are called tulips.

FIFTH CHILD: My mother has tulips, but some of them are yellow.

And, once again, a specific concept is on its way to being developed. Notice that in each conversation *one* concept is considered. Had the teacher tried to introduce the three concepts of blooming, spring, and tulips into one conversation many of the children would have come away confused. A sharing time for kindergarten and the primary grades is made up of a number of conversations. Each brief conversation should permit you to pick up one concept whose meaning can be extended. For many it may be the initial contact with an idea. You need to direct your comments in each conversation towards one concept and avoid latching on to tempting, auxiliary ideas as well.

Sharing time also should aid the young child develop confidence in what he has to say and in speaking before an audience. If the setting is informal—preferably a circle of children where some are on chairs and the rest sitting on the floor, with each child speaking from his own place—the conditions are good for encouraging such confidence. Confidence is sure to grow in a non-threatening situation.

Repeatedly successful sharing times will also help a child plan and carry out future conversations not only in the classroom setting but in other real-life situations. However, if not carefully guided by the teacher, sharing time may encourage a child to ramble and to bring unnecessary chatter to the classroom. Your reactions will influence each child's growing oral ability. Your genuine reactions should occur after the type of sharing that is of value: sharing that leads to positive learning such as vocabulary development, to social studies awareness, to sensitivity to numbers, to curiosity in the arts. It is best to employ rather noncommittal reactions to sharing that is merely gossip, retelling of television programs or movies, and unplanned talk thought of on the spur of the moment.

Sometimes it may become necessary to be quite clear about *no* television tales. What I mean are the blow by blow details of television programs given with such precision that it is as though you have viewed the program. Usually children should be sharing something far more personal than a favorite TV episode. You should not, however, discourage all experiences gained from seeing television, for there are documentaries and special dramatizations especially for children, and they can provide worthwhile material for sharing and discussing.

It may also be necessary to discourage, quite explicitly, the "stuff" that some children hurriedly pick up as they dash out of the house in an attempt to have something for sharing time. In such a situation, as well as when children give television recitals, your best reaction usually is one of very mild, though polite, interest. When such reactions are contrasted with your genuine enthusiasm for the kinds of sharing you hope will be repeated, you will be establishing standards which stress forethought and planning, and yet you will not actually be prescribing these standards.

Another talking time, similar to the sharing period, can prove quite valuable at the close of the school day when students are ready to go home. In an informal setting, preferably grouped in a conversational circle, the children can evaluate their day. What did I learn today? What did I do today? What problems did I have and how might they be solved? What do I need to make tomorrow a good day? End-of-the-day evaluations are helpful to children as they look toward future learning experiences at school.

Where to begin more formal talks by children

Somewhere along the way sharing needs to graduate into a more carefully prepared reporting. It may happen with many eight-year-olds on a very simple basis. Surely it will happen with most nine-year-olds. At this eight- and nine-year age level students should begin to plan what they will be saying and to practice their talks for someone, either at home or older children at school. Imagine the possibilities, as well as learnings, that could occur if boys and girls aged ten and eleven were to be scheduled regularly with individuals or small groups aged eight and nine to guide them in developing more effective oral talks.

Finally, nine-, ten-, and eleven-year-olds should begin, when ready, to prepare rather formal oral reports. These frequently can be based on current social studies and science units. The child who has had a background of experience talking purposefully to audiences will be ready to select his own topics for oral presentations.

You, the teacher, must assess your students early in the school year to determine where each one needs to begin. The preceding suggested age levels should remain *suggestions*. Your students may be ready for a different stage of development. It is quite possible that some eleven-year-olds will need to begin with simple sharing experiences: the opportunity must be provided. It is also quite possible that some seven-year-olds will be ready to prepare well thought out oral talks. Each child should feel comfortable. If, at all age levels, teachers begin the year with a brief time set aside each morning for sharing, it will be possible to identify those who find talking before an audience easy and those who are resourceful in choosing topics to share. With the older children you can offer the opportunity for those who would like to do so to prepare a special report for the class. When such first reports are presented the teacher will discover what instruction is needed to aid each student in progressing in his ability to speak to an audience.

What to consider when giving prepared oral talks

The speaker's fundamental considerations are his subject and his audience. He must have knowledge about his subject as well as a personal interest in it. With these prerequisities met, the speaker's attention must turn to his audience, for an effective speaker is one who has developed a perceptive sense of audience. He is eager to communicate and so is constantly questioning his efforts in terms of the listeners. Can he be heard? Are the words he has chosen making sense? How does he appear to those looking at him? What can be done to maintain and rekindle attention? If he were listening to himself what would be his reactions?

Before examining a host of other necessary considerations for successful prepared talks, let me suggest several ways to begin work on such oral presentations. After you and your students have had some opportunity to become acquainted, you might suggest that there are a number of ways that each of us can gain experience in talking before the group. Among them are (1) sharing personal experiences, (2) telling about some current news event, (3) reading or reciting a poem you have enjoyed as you were reading, (4) giving a talk about a book you recently finished, and (5) presenting an informational report. This list provides considerable variety and should appeal to all of your students. A useful means of organizing this activity is to display a chart where each child volunteers for the activity he will do as well as chooses the day to do it for the class. You may wish to set up this chart so that every child has an opportunity once each week to speak to the class, or you may prefer organizing this activity so that each child presents something once every two weeks. This would allow all students sufficient time to prepare, and might be more realistic in large classes, for when children volunteer to give a prepared talk to the class they should then receive the time necessary to be heard.

The chart might appear as Figure 5-2.

	SHARING	CURRENT EVENTS	POETRY	BOOKS	REPORTS
ORAL PRESENTATIONS					
MON.					
TUES.					
WED.					
THUR.					
FRI.					

Figure 5-2

Each child could have his own tagboard card with his name printed on it. He would place it in the slot that was appropriate for him. At a glance both teacher and students would know what oral presentations were on schedule for the day and the week. The slots could be made so that only a certain number of name tags would fit under each category. Another version of this chart is Figure 5-3.

ORAL PRESENTATIONS				
MON.	TUE.	WED.	THUR.	FRI.
————	————	————	————	————
————	————	————	————	————
————	————	————	————	————

Figure 5-3

Assign a different color of construction paper to each of the five categories. At the base of the chart provide a box with the cut pieces of colored paper. If blue represents a poetry presentation and a child chose to do one, he would write his name on one of the blue slips and place it in an available slot under one of the days of the week. You should determine the suitable number of slots for each day—three would mean 15 oral presentations for the week.

When I have used one of these charts to schedule oral experiences in my classroom, I have been surprised year after year to find a good number of individuals frequently selecting to present some poetry. Some of the students I have known who struggled with most of their academic work often were the ones who, with no suggestion from me, chose to memorize the poems they wished to share. Also, as the year progressed many children became quite effective in choosing a group of poems, rather than a single one, and their choices would generally cluster around a theme or the current weather or an approaching holiday. In my comments following such a presentation, I made a special point of praising the evident thought and preparation that went into the student's work.

One important suggestion if you decide to use this five category chart idea: get involved yourself. Choose an oral activity and take the plunge; put your marker on the chart. The first time you take the challenge to present some poetry you have memorized may prove to be an exciting and frightening experience, but it will be worth it. Your interest and enthusiasm will be catching. When you yourself do something you assign students you give it true status—it becomes important, worth doing, not just "something for the kids." *And* you will learn much about what is involved in preparing and presenting a book talk or informational report, or any of the other oral activities. Your personal understanding of the creating process will serve to make you a much more effective teacher.

Another way of beginning prepared oral talks with intermediate grade children is one that focuses on oral reports rather than on poetry presentations and current events. The first time this activity should probably be presented to the whole class, even though you must remember to individualize your evaluations of each child's results.

Select a nonfiction article, possibly from *My Weekly Reader* or the *Scholastic Newspapers,* both of which publications come once a week and are commonly received in schools. Usually news articles have excellent lead sentences, and you want to be sure the article you choose begins with a statement that is attention-grabbing. This is the point to be made: that an oral report must begin with an opening statement that catches the audience and makes them want to listen.

Then, for this first oral report, ask all the children to prepare a talk on anything they choose that can be divided into two main parts: who and what. To be an acceptable topic it must be one from which the student will be able to develop at least three sentences for each part. Here are *several typical examples:*

I. *My Pet*

    A. Who it is.

        1. My pet is a German police dog.
        2. His name is Boss because he usually gets his way.

     3. He is full grown and is taller than I am when he stands on his hind legs.

  B. What it does.

     1. Boss guards our house by barking fiercely whenever strangers come near.

     2. When I come home from school Boss likes to play with me.

     3. We wrestle and sometimes I make him chase a ball.

II. *Horses*

  A. Who are they?

     1. Horses are four-legged animals.

     2. There are palomino horses and appaloosa horses and lots of other kinds.

     3. You can recognize a horse by its long legs, mane, tail, and whinny.

  B. What do they do?

     1. Horses are used for racing and riding and pulling vehicles.

     2. They resist having a saddle on their backs at first and must be trained.

     3. Grains are eaten by horses.

If you ask each child to write out his statements you will be able to make suggestions that will aid him in developing an organized, though very simple, first talk. It might be helpful to use a duplicated form similar to Figure 5-4.

This form could be used by children once or twice, but more wisely, the form should be useful to each child until he is ready to expand into a more complex talk. Early in a child's experiences of prepared oral talks the idea of visual aids needs to be introduced. The use of visuals adds interest for the audience as well as being something to keep the novice speaker's hands constructively active. The danger for the young speaker is to get too many visuals. The ultimate in overloading a talk with visual aids is when someone finds a suitable filmstrip and proceeds to project *every* frame, reading the captions, and thus does not have to create any of the talk himself!

With the early talks where I concentrate on two main parts

PLANS FOR AN ORAL TALK

  I. Opening Statement

 II. Who

     A. 1st sentence
     B. 2nd sentence
     C. 3rd sentence

III. What

     A. 1st sentence
     B. 2nd sentence
     C. 3rd sentence

IV. Closing Statement

Figure 5-4

with a maximum of six sentences, I limit the use of visuals to one for each part of the who-what outline. Often these first efforts are crayon originals by the children, though they also use pictures from magazines or the library files, as well as objects of interest. As the students increase their talks to three- and four-part outlines (and more), then the number of visual aids can go up, too. The point is, the talk—what is being said—is most important; visuals should only serve to enhance the talk.

Throughout the year's work in developing increasingly effective oral talks there are a number of considerations that one should make, so let us return to those concerns.

First, *time* must be provided to work on these talks. It is not satisfactory to assign oral talks and expect them to be developed in free moments at school and at home. Students should have ready access to the teacher and to the librarian, as they seek source materials and as they organize the actual content of the talk. As talks take shape, the children must be given time to practice in the presence of one or two listeners. Eventually, I think some of the final talks of the year should include some practicing at home before parents or other siblings, but we must not expect the home to provide most of the instructional guidance necessary for growing success in preparing and presenting oral talks. Oral talks are usually not suitable as homework assignments.

Second, your students should be encouraged to use a *variety of sources* for information. There is little value in a child reciting from an entry in the encyclopedia. You will need to present the varied possibilities, and you may find the school librarian can help you. One effective way to introduce students to different sources is by having you occasionally prepare an oral talk yourself. At the completion of your talk, take time to analyze with the class your presentation as well as your preparation. A word of caution: limit your planned talks to a maximum of ten minutes (teachers have a tendency to talk too much!). In your analyses you can point out such sources as films, books other than encyclopedias, pictures, charts, newspapers, pamphlets, television, and other people.

Third, your students need some guidance in *taking notes* from their sources of information. Note-taking must not be a polite way for a student to copy, verbatim, everything he reads in an encyclopedia. Unless you present some skills for taking notes you will reap only stacks of handwritten copies of source books. I usually point out to my students that if they are simply going to present the same words that are found in a reference book, it would be easier and possibly more interesting just to let us read the book instead. This is especially true when it comes to written reports, for most of us would find it much pleasanter to read the printed page than the same text in a variety of styles of handwriting. I will have more to say concerning this subject in a later chapter on writing nonfiction.

Let us look more closely at note-taking for the purpose of oral talks. Notes for oral talks must be particularly brief, otherwise it is too easy a temptation to stand before a group and read. Your students need to be encouraged to write down only important words—I call them "cue" words because they *remind* you of a group of related words that you wish to express. A useful technique can be to have your students follow the Plan

For An Oral Talk outlined earlier in this chapter. After you have approved the plan, ask each student to turn the paper over and replace each sentence with as few words as are necessary to remind him of the whole sentence. It would be helpful to the children to present some concrete examples such as:

SENTENCE	CUE WORDS	FEWER CUE WORDS
1. My pet is a German police dog.	pet; German	German
2. When I come home from school Boss likes to play with me.	after school, plays with me	after; we play

Your examples should point out the possibilities of abbreviations and pseudo-shorthand symbols. We used to insist that students never use the plus sign for "and," but now we realize that such shortcuts are very appropriate to *notetaking*. You can also show examples that use fewer words and *different* ones from your basic sentence, yet serve as a quick reminder; for example, "we play" is a very brief but suitable cue for "likes to play with me."

Skill both in writing brief notes and in recognizing them as representing longer, more complete ideas will come with practice. It is also possible, on occasion, to have impromptu talks, for this encourages speakers to think on their feet and not to rely on any written text. Impromptu talks can also be fun if they are handled in an atmosphere of playful challenge. From a collection of topics I randomly call on different children, until everyone has had a chance to try speaking on the chosen subjects. No attempt to evaluate is necessary, and it could frighten the timid, less confident students to do so. Topics for these impromptu talks can come from current events both in the news and at school; they can be taken from familiar sayings; they can be contributed by the children themselves. For the timid or reluctant people I try to select topics which I feel they can handle with some success. Here are a few suggested topics:

Time Flies
Saint Patrick's Day

Eating Spaghetti
A Happy Moment
Flying a Kite
A Sad Moment
Don't Cry Over Spilt Milk
Travel to the Moon

Procedures for evaluation

Evaluation of prepared oral talks will be most helpful when it comes from the other students. From the very first, time should be taken after each talk for classmates to make comments regarding particular aspects that made the presentation interesting. There can be comments suggesting ideas for improvement the next time. I usually call on two children to make positive comments and two to make suggestions. It is often necessary to limit the number of children participating in evaluation simply because of the time it takes, especially if you are working with over 30 children. I also make evaluative comments, but it is best that those from the teacher are few and occur less and less often as the year progresses. It has been my practice to make written comments after each talk. These comments may be sent home if it is your practice to send home a regular communication regarding your school program, or they may be collected in each child's folder for reference at parent-teacher conferences.[1]

I often distribute to the class duplicated copies of the form I use for written comments, so that the speaker's classmates can also participate in this evaluation. I usually number these forms from one to five; that way one-fifth of the class evaluates each speaker. Figure 5-5 is a suggested form for a written evaluation.

The form I use varies from year to year, but it reflects the points I consider important, and these are determined from hearing the students' evaluative comments as well as from my own observations of the speakers. When I begin to use a printed form for recording comments I talk about each item with the

---

[1] For a description of a weekly letter I have sent home with the children I teach, *read* "Friday Letter" published in the *Elementary School Journal,* April 1963.

EVALUATION OF THE ORAL PRESENTATION
GIVEN BY _____

Subject Matter _____

Speaks clearly

      1) uh, and uh, well, etc.

Has eye contact with entire audience

Free of distracting movements

Has materials in order

Visuals shown so all could see

Other comments: _____

Figure 5-5

class and encourage ideas from the students to help clarify the various categories.

Oral presentations may also be tape recorded as a means of evaluation. This is an excellent procedure for students to follow in preparing their talks, for hearing themselves on tape will help many people improve their talks before they give them to the full audience. If you should become overwhelmed by the sheer numbers of students prepared to talk and the number of minutes it will take, and if the hall or an auxiliary room is available, you can have some of the children give their talks to a smaller audience while you maintain your classroom. If this smaller group uses the tape recorder for this purpose, you can listen after school and make your written comments. These small audience groups will appeal especially to timid or shy individuals. The knowledge that their talks are being recorded serves as a disciplinary control for children meeting in a place other than the classroom.

IN SUMMARY

1. It is essential to provide time for and genuine interest in all children who wish to share experiences.

2. Sharing time at its best is a vehicle for establishing and developing concepts.
3. Sharing time in the early grades may serve to increase self-confidence when speaking before a group.
4. More formal, structured talks should begin on an individual basis only when each child shows readiness.
5. Preparing oral talks generally should be a school activity, not a homework assignment, for the teacher needs to be involved in guiding such preparation.
6. The entire class should be involved in the process of evaluation, which must emphasize positive, constructive comments.

BULLETIN BOARD IDEA

COMMENT: If you have access to a camera, it would be interesting to take pictures of your students posing to illustrate each of the above types of poor speaker. Otherwise, children might make drawings or find suitable pictures in commercial magazines.

6

Building Teamwork with Choral Reading

Choral reading is a language arts activity that can accomplish a number of necessary and related experiences, for it permits the introduction of many fine poems (and the poets responsible, as well); it allows poetry to be heard, not merely read silently—and this is a must when bringing children and poetry together; it affords a natural setting for good poetry to be heard over and over, which is essential because a poem needs repeating in order to savor the flow of the language and the thoughts; it provides an opportunity for students to work together both in planning and practicing as well as in performing; and it offers a profitable experience for children who are having difficulty in the areas of reading and speaking.

Briefly, let us define choral reading as speaking in groups of varying sizes, using poetry or other literary works. There can be solo parts, but they should fit within the framework of a group. Choral speaking makes possible a variety of ways of interpreting moods, expressions, and meanings. In addition, choral speaking encourages clearer speech and provides considerable practice (but, oh, so pleasant) in speaking clearly, particularly for the child from a "disadvantaged" background whose opportunities to read fine literature and to speak effectively in school settings have been frequently limited.

Variations for the primary-aged child

In the very first years of school young children will delight in the rhythms of nursery rhymes. Their delight should find expression, for they need not be just passive listeners as a teacher reads from one of the many beautiful, recent, editions of the Mother Goose verses. The rhymes are usually short, generally quite catchy, and easy to learn. No concerted effort is necessary to "teach" rhymes to young children, for frequent exposure seems to result in spontaneous memorization. How few times it takes for children to hear, "Hickory dickory dock, the mouse ran up the clock. The clock struck one, the mouse ran down, hickory dickory dock," before they are saying it with the teacher.

Sharing simple rhymes and good, brief poems with children in their early school years must be a natural, frequent part of most days. If the teacher presents them in a relaxed, pleasant atmosphere, one where the teacher can smile easily and genuinely enjoy the music of such verse, the children will find it comfortable and pleasant first to mouth some of the words softly and then joyfully to speak all of the words aloud.

As the young child begins to collect a repertoire of speakable verse, there are numerous possibilities of enhancing this oral-literary experience. Perhaps as a beginning one could encourage some added physical responses. In "Hickory Dickory Dock" I often sit with the children and begin by asking them to count softly *one, two, three, four, one, two, three, four*. I ask them to continue counting, and then I say "Hickory Dickory Dock" to the accompaniment of their counting. Then I hold up one hand, resting the elbow on my knee and suggest the children do the same. This time we count aloud the four-four pattern and move our hands back and forth in proper rhythm, so that our hands are working as metronomes. Once again, as the children count aloud and move their hands, I repeat the verse. At this point there are several slight variations that can be done with "Hickory Dickory Dock." Perhaps half of the children will count and the rest recite the verse, with *everyone* acting as metronomes. Or I may be the only counter while all of the children do the reciting. One necessary consideration: do not allow physical movement or counting to distract from the words of the verse.

"Sing a Song of Sixpence" tells a somewhat more complicated story and also lends itself to a choral recitation. Often the children are quite familiar with singing this rhyme, so I suggest we try saying it. The second stanza has several ideas which can be simply acted by the children *as they are sitting.* Each idea should be introduced separately. Begin with the final line, "When down came a blackbird and snipped off her nose." I usually ask the children to try saying "blackbird" in a scary or mean voice. This is fun and each time we go through the verse they are eager to interpret this word. Follow with "The King was in his counting house, counting out his money." The boys and girls can each make the motions, in front of themselves, of stacking various coins, so when you recite the whole verse pause at this point for the children to have time to do the counting motions. Then for, "The Queen was in the parlor eating bread and honey," you might suggest the hand movement over the stomach that indicates that the food tastes good. For the next line, "The maid was in the garden hanging out the clothes," each child should take time to pantomime the act of lifting a garment up to a clothesline and clipping clothespins to it. Finally, focus again on the final line and have the children try saying the word "snipped" in a clipped, cutting voice.

Let me repeat that this experience was done as the children *remained sitting,* yet it was in effect adding some slight dramatization to the choral speaking. Choral speaking at any age level does not need elaborate dramatization support. The words themselves, and the clarity and unity with which they are spoken are the most important aspects here and must not become distracted by dramatizing.

Ways to approach choral reading with older children

It would seem wise to move away from even the simple dramatic movements when working with third graders, and by fourth grade all concern should be on effective ways of speaking with no bodily actions.

Choral reading should be a pleasant activity, not one designed solely to improve one's individual speaking ability. In fact, this aspect should be a by-product of many experiences of speaking poetry.

For the intermediate grade child the selection of poetry continues to be of utmost importance. Verse that appeals to the sense of sound is particularly effective. Also poems that create unusual moods and poems that tell a story both appeal to the older child. At Halloween "The Goblin" [1] by Rose Fyleman is suitable for all ages. It is one that is so easily learned that there is no need to duplicate copies. Once you have recited the poem for the class, encourage the students to join you, but remind them to watch you quite closely, for you will signal different individuals or groups to say certain parts. Here is the poem with suggested parts:

> ALL: A goblin lives in our house,
> In our house, in our house,
> A goblin lives in our house
> All the year long.

ONE CHILD: He bumps
ANOTHER CHILD: And he jumps
A THIRD CHILD: And he thumps
A FOURTH CHILD: And he stumps.
A FIFTH CHILD: He knocks
A SIXTH CHILD   And he rocks

---

[1] Rose Fyleman, *Picture Rhymes from Foreign Lands* (Philadelphia: J. B. Lippincott Co., Copyright 1935, 1963).

A SEVENTH CHILD: And he rattles at the locks.

ALL: *(repeat verse)*

Each time you go through this, point to different children. Encourage the seventh child to "make those locks really rattle with your voice." Later point to various small groups of children to say one of the phrases, "in our house," for this will give the effect of goblins being in many different houses. Also, the word "goblin" can be said mysteriously each time, perhaps in a breathy manner.

Another poem that can be enjoyed at Halloween is "A Halloween Chant"[2] by D. Matthews. Divide the class into two groups. Suggest that one group try to sound high and squeaky while the other groups try for a low and mysterious sound. Here is the poem with suggestions for the two parts:

> *(high)*   This is the night,
> *(low)*   This dark, eerie night,
> *(high)*   The only night in the year
> *(low)*   We come from our holes
>   Like dreary, black moles,
> ALL: And walk on the earth without fear.
> *(low)*   We're witches and gnomes,
>   And ghosts without homes;
> ALL: We're goblins and banshees and elves!
> *(low)*   We're spooks from the graves,
>   And bats from the caves,
> ALL: We're almost afraid of ourselves!
> *(high)*   With shriekings and moans
> *(low)*   And rattling of bones,
> ALL: We'll laugh and we'll wail and we'll weep!
> *(high)*   But the hours fly by!
>   Dawn creeps to the sky,
> ALL: And we must return to our sleep.
>   *(long drawn out sigh)*

Here is a poem that tells a story and will hold considerable appeal, especially for the boys.

---

[2] D. Matthews, "A Halloween Chant," *Grade Teacher* Magazine.

JOE'S SNAKE STORY [3]

SOLO BOY:	Once I went for a walk in the woods.
	I walked and walked and walked and walked.
ALL:	Stop, Joe, you're tired by now
	With your walk . . . walk . . . walk.
SOLO BOY:	I sure was tired so I sat down to rest.
	And what did I sit on but a big old snake
	About a mile long and thick as a fire plug!
ALL:	Why, Joe, what an awful snake . . .
	Did you run . . . run . . . run?
SOLO BOY:	No! The big old snake began to jerk and jerk
	And wrinkle up his face and go,
SOLO GIRL:	"Uh, uh, uh . . . Ker-choo!"
SOLO BOY:	Because ants had run across his nose.
	And . . . when . . . he . . . sneezed . . . !
ALL:	Careful, Joe, you have us scared
	Stiff . . . stiff . . . stiff.
SOLO BOY:	When . . . he . . . sneezed . . . he sneezed so hard
	He blew a cow right out of the field!
	He blew a roof right off a house!
	He blew all the water out of the creek!
	And he blew a road right into the next state!
	That woke up all the other snakes who were
	His aunts and uncles and brothers and sisters
	And Mom and Pop and even his great-great grand-
	father.
	And they came rolling and tumbling and hissing
	All around my bare feet.
ALL:	Oh, Joe, we're on the edge
	Of our seats . . . seats . . . seats.
SOLO BOY:	So I began to run on my big top toes,
	Right over the backs of all those snakes.
	And that tickled them in their ribs
	So much they had to giggle and laugh.
	They all laughed so they couldn't get
	Their breath to chase me.
	They couldn't even hiss.
	So I ran home and locked the door
	And all the windows,
	Even those on the third floor.

_____

[3] Ruth Eckman, "Joe's Snake Story," *Grade Teacher* Magazine.

ALL: Golly, Joe, we're glad you're home
              And safe . . . safe . . . safe.

                                        —*Ruth Eckman*

Children in the intermediate grades should be encouraged to
bring in poems they would like to do chorally. Either as individuals or as groups, they can also determine how a particular
poem might be broken for solo voices and group participation.
Involving the students in selection and arranging is likely to
increase their interest in choral reading.

Another way of involving the older students is by encouraging them to volunteer to be directors for different poems. The
selection of a director should be made strictly from the volunteers. A director should help the speakers by giving appropriate
signals for entrances. This is usually done quite simply with
some hand or finger motion to indicate who is to speak. Occasionally the director may want to indicate an increase in
volume. Each director should develop his own signals, but they
must remain simple. Avoid overly dramatic arm waving.

Another basis for choral speaking besides using poetry is
utilizing original prose selections of the children. I have had
successful results in developing Christmas programs around a
choral presentation. I remember the year I finally found myself
very tired of hearing young children struggle to read the King
James Version of the Christmas story—beautiful words *not* intended to be read aloud by a ten- or eleven-year-old. I asked
one of my students who had enjoyed writing all autumn to try
writing the basic Christmas story in her own words. The results
were delightfully child-like, clear, and to the point. We used
her prose rendering of the Christmas story as the material for
the sixth graders to speak chorally while children from the
other rooms either dramatized certain scenes or sang songs
fitting the particular point in the choral reading.

Another year I asked a group of fourth, fifth, and sixth graders
to try to develop a Christmas alphabet. From the pooled results
we used several ideas for each letter as material for a very simple
choral reading, which in turn served as a structure on which to

develop pantomime dramatizations and musical presentations by other children, resulting in a most effective yet simply performed Christmas program.

Suggested material for choral reading

There is no end to the possible materials, both prose and poetry, both original and already-created, that can be suitable for choral reading. Here are only a few suggestions—material I have found effective with children:

GRIZZLY BEAR [4]

If you ever, ever, ever meet a grizzly bear,
You must never, never, never ask him where
He is going,
Or what he is doing;
For if you ever, ever, dare
To stop a grizzly bear,
You will never meet another grizzly bear.

—Mary Austin

A YELL FOR YELLOW [5]

Yellow, yellow, hello, yellow:
Welcome to forsythia and dandelions in Spring,
To buttercups and goldenrod and warblers on the wing.

Yellow, yellow, mellow yellow:
Yellow as new wood, yellow as wheat,
Yellow as cornbread sweet to eat.

Yellow, yellow, let's bellow yellow:
Yellow monkeys peeling bananas!
Yellow chickens playing pianos!
Butterflies, goldfish, cat's eyes!

---

[4] Mary Austin, "Grizzly Bear," *The Children Sing in the Far West* (Boston: Houghton Mifflin Company).

[5] Eve Merriam, "A Yell for Yellow," *There Is No Rhyme for Silver* (New York: Atheneum Publishers, copyright © 1962).

Yellow, yellow, yell on yellow:
Yellow is a lemon smell, it tingles like a sneeze,
Tickles like the sunshine, jingles like a breeze!

—Eve Merriam

WASHING [6]

What is all this washing about,
Everyday, week in, week out?
From getting up till going to bed,
I'm tired of hearing the same thing said.
Whether I'm dirty or whether I'm not.
Whether the water is cold or hot,
Whether I like or whether I don't,
Whether I will or whether I won't,
"Have you washed your hands, and washed your face?"
I seem to *live* in the washing-place.

Whether I go for a walk or ride,
As soon as I put my nose inside
The door again, there's someone there
With a sponge and soap, and a lot they care
If I have something better to do,
"Now wash your face and your fingers too."

Before a meal is even begun,
And after ever a meal is done,
It's time to turn on the waterspout,

Please, what *is* all this washing about?

—John Drinkwater

Dangers to be alert to

A most serious danger is the easy tendency for choral reading of poetry to become sing-song. This can be avoided somewhat by careful selection, but even so, when a poem has a definite rhyming pattern it is difficult not to produce a sing-song effect. The important point is to concentrate on the meaning of the words and phrases. Use the commas and periods and other marks of punctuation to guide the reading, for usually the sing-

---

[6] John Drinkwater, "Washing," *More About Me* (London: Wm. Collins Sons and Co., Ltd.).

song effect indicates lack of proper phrasing. Ask the children to help decide what words really are important and deserve emphasis.

Another possible danger is allowing choral reading to be totally program-directed. That is, the idea of a finished performance takes on too much importance. A final performance can be quite appropriate but each practice session should be a pleasant, satisfying experience. It is better to end with a program as a natural outgrowth of a series of informal choral speaking sessions than to decide ahead of time that a choral reading program must occur.

A third danger has been mentioned earlier and bears repeating. Gestures generally lead to over-dramatization and detract from the delivery. Avoid gestures and concentrate on clarity of speech and sincerity of expression.

Finally, choose only first-rate verse, and do not be enticed by timely but banal or cheaply sentimental poetry. Turn to such fine collections as the Arbuthnot anthology *Time For Poetry,* to Mother Goose, and to many parts of the Bible.

Procedures for evaluation

Each child should withdraw temporarily from a group practice to be a listener. In this way the children will gain a fuller idea of the potential impact of choral speaking as well as serve as their own critics.

If you have divided your class into several speaking groups then each group can become an evaluator of the other groups. An advantage of this procedure is that those listening are not as likely to be familiar with the text of the selection and so will be able to point out words or phrases that are not spoken clearly enough to be understood.

Through the use of a tape recorder, evaluation can occur more frequently and at various times during the day. Individuals or groups can listen to a tape, if the recorder is equipped with earphones, at any time and not disturb the rest of the class. It is beneficial to save samples of recorded choral speaking done throughout a school year. Near the end of the year the students can listen to the accumulated samples and discuss their progress.

IN SUMMARY

1. Choral speaking is a most satisfying way to meet many fine literary works, to work together for a common goal, and to develop one's love for our language.
2. To be most successful, choral reading must be experienced in an atmosphere of exploration where the students are personally involved in the selection of materials, the choral arrangements, and the evaluation of the results.

Bibliography

ARBUTHNOT, MAY HILL, *Children and Books* (3rd ed.). Glenview, Illinois: Scott, Foresman and Company, 1964. This valuable resource contains an excellent chapter on verse choirs. It includes guidelines to follow as well as specific suggestions of poetry to use.

ARBUTHNOT, MAY HILL, editor, *Time for Poetry*. Illustrated by Arthur Paul. Glenview, Illinois: Scott, Foresman and Company, 1952. Here is a most useful collection of poetry. Many of the poems are suitable for choral reading and contain suggestions for such use.

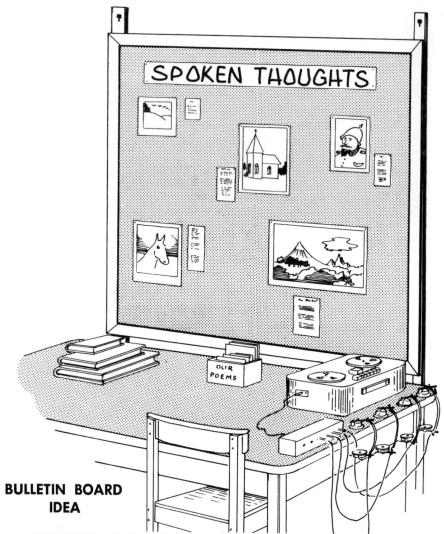

BULLETIN BOARD IDEA

COMMENT: A bulletin board devoted to choral speaking might well serve as a center for collecting useful materials. On a bulletin board entitled SPOKEN THOUGHTS, as above, there could be displayed suitable selections of poetry attractively mounted and placed near related illustrations. On a table beneath the board there could be a box containing other poems, duplicated and mounted on pieces of cardboard (to facilitate handling). The students should be encouraged to choose poems to prepare for the class as choral readings. Also on the table there could be several volumes of poetry (frequently changed throughout the year) and a tape recorder equipped with a listening post.

7

How to Develop Effective Listening Habits

There is a difference between hearing and listening

Children probably engage in the activity of hearing more than in listening. The range of hearing is from very vague awareness of sounds to the superficial reception of specific sounds. An example is the child, intently watching a television program in a room where adults are talking, who is not really aware of what they are saying, while those same adults, who realize that the television is on, are giving their prime attention to their own conversation. Actually, in each instance both hearing and listening are taking place. Listening involves concentration, purpose, and involvement. It may be more difficult today to be effective listeners, for our daily life is bombarded with sounds: a radio going in the kitchen, teenagers singing and dancing to records in the front room, mother talking on the phone in the hall, the dishwasher swishing, spraying, and humming in the kitchen with the automatic washer and dryer doing something similar in the utility room, and the television running on in the den. Sound familiar? This is only a description of some of the sounds at home. Think about the sounds of school, which actually is not a quiet haven of silent study since the teacher is talking to a small group, individuals are visiting, other classes are moving in the halls, bells are ringing, there are interruptions of the public address system, the aquarium is bubbling, someone is grinding the pencil sharpener, drawers and desk tops are banging, people are coughing and sneezing. Oh, yes, school is a world of sound!

Perhaps the preceding paragraph is not so much an explanation of why it is difficult to be a good listener today but is, instead, evidence of the facility with which we human beings do, in fact, *listen* to those sounds which have a meaning for us. If mother allowed those countless home sounds to disturb her she would not be able to become engrossed in her telephone conversation. In terms of our classrooms, students do *listen* to that which seems important while they simply *hear* the other sounds around them.

Do students and teachers listen?

Unfortunately, our students may hear us, but how often do they find it necessary to listen to us? We have a tendency to establish oral routines which boys and girls recognize as almost meaningless. Among the routines here are three of the most pervasive: (1) endless cautions—to walk quietly and to speak softly, (2) lectures on how important it is to learn something because "you will need to know this when you grow up," and (3) the mass of daily directions which usually are repeated two or three times.

When cautions are expressed they frequently are accompanied with threats of punishment, threats that are often made and seldom carried out. "When you grow up" lectures generally reach deaf ears, for children do not seriously see themselves as future adults but tend to reason, "If what I am learning is not important to me *now* then I do not need to listen to what the teacher is saying." Finally, the time-honored teacher habit of repeating directions does much to condition children to the futility of listening. They are inclined to think, "As long as teacher is going to tell us what to do over and over, I can use this time for more interesting activity. I will tune in later, and if I miss something I will ask after everyone else starts working."

We teachers must make an extensive effort to condition our students to expect directions to be given *only once*. I have found this a most difficult habit to break. But I also have found that students who do not expect repetitions of directions do listen carefully. Also, when teachers intend to give directions only once they become more thoughtful about what must be said so that it will be an articulate message.

Just as students learn not to listen to their teachers, teachers may also set a poor example by failing to really listen to their students. It is difficult to give careful attention to individuals in a classroom of over 30, but unless teachers show by example that what others have to say is worthy of thoughtful listening, they will fail in their subsequent efforts to aid boys and girls in becoming better listeners. Listen to yourself, perhaps with the aid of a tape recorder, and determine when you are worth listening to and when you are not.

Suggestions for becoming more effective listeners

Assuming that you are endeavoring to teach your students how to be honest, sincere listeners, there are some specific ways to improve their listening skills. Begin by giving more accurate directions. Think through your directions before saying them, and whenever possible, try to follow your own directions before asking children to. There are activities with simple directions that are useful in developing listening as well as fun to do, and I will mention several, but it is easy to play "direction" games and then forget to improve the *real* and *necessary* directions that one must give daily, so do not depend just upon games to help children follow directions.

A. Activities for Following Directions

1. Draw simple maps. In precise statements direct students to make a map. For example: (*a*) make a box in the lower left

hand corner; (*b*) mark it with the word "school"; (*c*) draw a line from the school along the bottom of the paper to the center; (*d*) draw a circle at this point; (*e*) mark it with the word "store"; (*f*) draw a triangle in the top right hand corner; (*g*) mark it with the words "Mary's house"; (*h*) draw a line from the store to Mary's house; etc.

Begin with very easy maps and progress to more complex ones. This is a suitable activity to tie in with a social studies unit on maps and globes.

2. Give walking directions. Various children can have turns being the director who tries to be very precise in telling another student where to walk. For example, (*a*) John, stand up; (*b*) face the front of the classroom; (*c*) walk forward; (*d*) stop; (*e*) face the windows; (*f*) walk forward; (*g*) stop, etc.

Other movements can be included such as kneel, crawl, wave, extend an arm.

3. Cut, paste, and draw. Plan a simple activity where you can give concise directions for children who have been provided with scissors, paste, crayons, and construction paper. After the children demonstrate success in following very elementary directions such as: (*a*) cut a red square; (*b*) paste it in the center of the white paper; (*c*) use a green crayon to outline the square; (*d*) make a series of outlines with the green crayon—then you can go on to different art activities of paper folding and weaving which require preliminary basic directions.

B. Other Listening Activities

1. Listen to a short story with specific purposes set up beforehand. Create your own story or use stories written by the children. Ask students to listen for one or two purposes; do not complicate matters by asking them to think about too many purposes. Some purposes for listening to a story might be: (*a*) who was lost in the woods, or other appropriate "who" questions; (*b*) where was the space ship when the storm ended, or other suitable "where" questions; (*c*) "when" questions; and (*d*) "what" questions.

2. Listen to sounds and ideas of words. Reading aloud to children can be quite helpful in stimulating better listening. Select stories that are exciting, compelling, compassionate, and well-written. Also choose poetry that highlights sound and color words. (See Chapter 1 for suggestions about selecting suitable material to read aloud as well as comments about presenting oral reading effectively.)

3. Listen and react to oral talks. (See Chapter 5.) Consider having older children prepare talks that would be appropriate for younger children.

4. Listen to music. Attending children's concerts, tuning in on FM radio stations, and listening to selected records are all ways of including music in your listening program. To have successful listening experiences with music you will want to point out specific features and passages of each composition for the children. For instance, you might suggest they listen for certain instruments that introduce different parts of the music, or that they listen for recognizable themes such as the one that always introduces Peter or the one representing the wolf in Prokofiev's work "Peter and the Wolf." Music that tells a story is very effective for developing listening awareness. Grieg's "Peer Gynt Suite" and Dukas' "Sorcerers' Apprentice" are two possibilities. One should also introduce music that is not necessarily based upon a story. Such music will permit children to imagine their own stories. Several useful selections are Ponchielli's "Dance of the Hours" and Smetana's "The Moldau." The music of Leroy Anderson, a contemporary composer, is delightful, and children enjoy attempting to guess the titles of such selections as his "Waltzing Cat," "Syncopated Clock," and "Typewriter Song." The suggestions students have after listening to his "Sandpaper Ballet" are usually charming as well as unexpected. Marching melodies including those by Sousa and the more recent "Seventy-Six Trombones" by Meredith Willson are enjoyed by children of all ages.

5. Another aspect of music listening occurs when students create their own songs. An open invitation may be enough to bring forth original compositions, but you may have more success if you can include yourself in the early stages. When I am fortunate enough to have access to a piano I occasionally pick out a few notes and play them in a repeated pattern. Then I comment to the class, "This sounds like the beginning of a song. Can you think of words to fit?" Sometimes, after this introductory exposure, the students work together with me to compose a complete song, but more often I leave them with the suggestion, "Perhaps some of you would like to get together on your own and write the rest of the song." The Christmas song, Figure 7-1, was created in this way. I was responsible for the first line of music, for which the class decided upon the words. Afterwards a group of nine or ten girls met for several noon periods to write the remainder, including the words and the harmony. There is no doubt that children throughout the school listened intently to the finished piece. In fact, the group of girls became a girls' chorus and were frequently invited to sing in other rooms as well as in the community, and this song became their most popular tune even long after Christmas. Here was listening with real personal purpose.

Figure 7-1

6. A third aspect of music listening is in the presentation of vocal selections where it is necessary to listen carefully to understand the meaning of the words. Especially suited for this are ballads which tell stories through many verses. Folk music includes such ballads as "Lord Randall," "Cockles and Mussels," and "The Arkansas Traveler," but there are contemporary ballads in which today's children may show even more interest. One song written during World War II tells a dramatic story of a young hero, and I have found it to be one that intermediate-aged children listen to closely and with genuine sensitivity. It is "Rodger Young" by Frank Loesser. Encourage your students to bring in recordings of songs that tell stories, and share them with the class.

You may have been surprised at this sortie into music, but I am convinced that here is both a pleasant and a useful way to sharpen one's listening powers. I also believe that tomorrow's adults will have a greater opportunity, more than any previous generation, to spend time with the arts, and so we owe it to our children to aid them in becoming sensitive, perceptive music listeners.

In returning to the problem of helping children become better skilled in listening to the spoken word, this section will close with a few guidelines for setting suitable conditions for good listening.

1. There must be adequate physical conditions. This means comfort in terms of temperature, lighting, and seating. Also, fatigued children tend to be poor listeners. You may not be able

to control the amount of rest your students have at home, but you can minimize the problem by being alert to the class day you have developed in terms of balancing fatiguing activities with relaxing ones. Finally, suitable physical conditions include auditory requisites of adequate volume and tonal quality.

2. The listening experience needs to be adjusted to the general interest and intellectual level of the children.
3. The purpose of the listening experience must be understood.
4. There should be opportunities for expressing one's views along with listening to the contributions of others.
5. Visual and auditory distractions need to be minimized.
6. There must be an abundance and variety of types of experiences.
7. Good rapport is essential between speaker and listeners.

How to measure listening ability

For such activities as drawing simple maps, taking directions for walking, cut-paste-draw, and listening to stories with specific purposes, you can use a simple check list such as the following:

Name of child _____

Date _____

Drawing Simple Maps

	Listening Success	
1st direction	YES	NO
2nd direction	YES	NO
3rd direction	YES	NO
(etcetera)		

Such listening activities should be repeated frequently during the year and a check list marked each time for every child. A collection of these should prove useful as you assess your students' individual progress.

Subjective evaluation surely will occur when you read aloud to your students. You will observe their reactions, their questions, and their comments. Also, in discussing music listening experiences you will employ subjective judgments.

Above all, take time to evaluate yourself as to how effectively you communicate with your students. Perhaps a simple check list for your own personal use would be helpful:

Date _____

What I talked about _____

How long did I talk _____

How successful was I in communicating:

     Very_____ Moderate_____ Fair_____ Poor_____

What might I do to improve _____

_____

If you would keep such a record of yourself at least once a week you would be surprised at how your own improvement would be reflected in the increased care your students took to listen.

IN SUMMARY

1. All of us listen (or hear) more than we read or write, and probably more than we speak.
2. We are selective listeners and as teachers we must maximize the worthwhile opportunities for listening.
3. Teachers have a dual responsibility: to listen to (not just hear) their students and to plan what is said so that students find it worth listening.
4. Plan classroom experiences carefully so that children have consistent, sequential experiences in listening.
5. Take time to evaluate with children their progress in learning to be better listeners.

Bibliography

DUKER, SAM, *Listening: Readings*. New York: The Scarecrow Press, 1966. A fine collection of papers on listening including research, teaching suggestions for the elementary and secondary schools, and measuring listening ability.

RUSSELL, DAVID H., and ELIZABETH F. RUSSELL, *Listening Aids*

Through the Grades. New York: Teachers College Columbia University, 1959. An older publication but full of practical ideas.

WAGNER, GUY, MAX HOSIER, and MILDRED BLACKMAN, *Listening Games: Building Listening Skills with Instructional Games.* Darien, Connecticut: *Grade Teacher* Magazine, 1962. Another book of practical ideas. The introductory chapter provides an excellent explanation of the importance and use of listening games.

Linda R.	Record #5 9/20	Tape #4 9/30
John W.	Tape #3 10/12	Record #5 10/19
Roy L.	Taped song 10/2	Created lesson
Mary J.	Created lesson 10/4	Record
June M.	Record #12 9/18	
___ll J	Created lesson	

OUR
LISTENING
POST

CHECK YOUR
LISTENING SKILLS

OUR PROGRESS

OUR
AUDIO
TAPES

BULLETIN BOARD IDEA

COMMENT: Arrange a table beneath a bulletin board with (1) a collection of audio tapes developed by you and the students, (2) a variety of phonograph records, (3) question sheets for guiding and checking one's listening skills, (4) a tape recorder, and (5) a phonograph. On the bulletin board place a chart with all the students' names and places to note the dates when individuals participated in a listening skill activity. It might be of added interest to encourage students to use the post to design their own listening skills-checks by providing a blank tape and paper for the students to compose questions for other students to use when listening to these original assignments.

How to Say What We Mean: Building Word Power

Have a love affair with words

Words do matter. Those you use in your speech and writing should be carefully selected. Words your children use should reflect a growing concern for appropriate selection. When, during a sharing time, Johnny says, "We had a nice time at the beach," and in his creative writing he records, "Spring is a nice time," you have a strong signal that Johnny may be word-poor. "Nice" Johnny needs help. He needs an environment rich in words, peopled with those who care what ideas are expressed and how that expression is accomplished. If your personal reading includes both adult fiction and nonfiction from books, magazines, and newspapers you can be on the lookout for new vocabulary that will enrich one's writing. Then, if you share *periodically* with children your continually growing interest in vocabulary, your class will be well on its way to having a "love affair" with words.

This can be accomplished by talking about what you have read, posting vivid words and phrases on the chalkboard or on a special bulletin board, and by discussing with children various ways of expressing a single idea. And, of course, your daily conversations with children should reflect your wealth of vocabulary. We tend to oversimplify our choice of words when we talk with children, believing that we aid communication with them, when really we should be providing a vocabulary that causes each child to reach up. We so often teach in our reading classes about the importance of using context around a strange word to determine its meaning, but then we forget to use strange words in meaningful contexts when we talk. I know a third-grade teacher who, when the situation demanded, would say to her class, "There is too much competition of voices so I cannot hear what Mary is saying to me." By her consistent use of the word *competition* in this context, she gave that word a particular meaning without ever defining it for the children.

Ways to develop word awareness

In addition to using new words and talking about them in incidental conversations, there are a number of ways you can sharpen each child's awareness of new ways to express ideas.

A most fitting time to start is when you are reading aloud to the children. When you select carefully the pieces of literature to read to your children you will be providing an excellent basis for stimulating word awareness. For example, when I was reading Marguerite Henry's *Benjamin West and His Cat Grimalkin,*[1] I came across numerous images that were worth commenting upon. Some of them verge on the trite or cliché, but often the cliché that is a wornout expression for the adult is freshly vivid for the child. It is a starting place, and you can go beyond it when you recognize that an expression has become a cliché for any particular child and that the child is ready to reach out for new images to say the same idea.

In *Benjamin West* the boy's father, a Quaker innkeeper, was once described in this manner: "By night the guests hovered around him like bees after honey." I commented on the author's

---

[1] Marguerite Henry, *Benjamin West and His Cat Grimalkin,* illustrated by Wesley Dennis (New York: Bobbs-Merrill, 1947).

use of an image that helped us see more accurately what she was describing, and then I suggested that each child notice things about the room and school trying to create images. As I read on in Miss Henry's book we noted such word pictures as, "Often he caught himself humming like a teakettle," and "William Williams was a little cricket of a man," and "The words tumbled out like water over a mill wheel." Soon we became very conscious of images. Children discovered them in their own pleasure reading, and many began creating their own which they collected on paper in their notebooks. One day I had the opportunity to point out the need to be original, and in this way I introduced the idea of the cliché. The clocks in our building had gone haywire for over a week. On this day I was across the hall for a few minutes with another group of children when suddenly we were aware that the clocks were being adjusted. The hands of the clock moved rapidly until they were correctly set. When I returned to my own class I commented on the setting of the clocks and I shared with them what the other children had said. Their comment had been, "Gee, time sure flies." Now, for one child to say this was an accurate image, but no child said anything different. Various children simply repeated the image, "Time surely flies." I suggested to my class that there must be other appropriate images to describe the rapid movement of the clock hands, and they eagerly began groping for new expressions. Thus we began to realize what causes a cliché and the need to avoid saying an idea in a way that many others have already used.

The literature period, when the teacher reads aloud to children, is an excellent place to help develop word awareness. Besides talking about an author's use of words, you can develop bulletin boards and charts to spotlight new vocabulary. These can include quotations from literature that describe people, feelings, scenes, and activities. Such a bulletin board can change its emphasis continually. For instance, one week you might post quotations from various sources of ways authors effectively describe food and its preparation. The next week you might use literary material describing clothes; another week would be devoted to descriptions of sounds; then a week on descriptions of the weather. Such a bulletin board could continue throughout a school year, and it should successfully spark your children's awareness to the potential of our language.

Your children can also develop a section in their notebooks, or separate folders or booklets, for which you regularly hand out duplicated pages containing quotations from good children's literature from sources you have discovered and those contributed by the children. There should also be pages which have quotations you have selected from the children's own creative writing which illustrate unique ways of using words.

A vital reference for your classroom is the dictionary. Ideally every child would have a dictionary at his desk. But there should also be an "adult" dictionary in the classroom as well as a thesaurus and a synonym dictionary. Children must learn that a dictionary is far more useful than serving just as a source for correct spelling. Its service as a definition source is much more important. Do not overlook the potential for finding many new uses for "old" words by referring to the dictionary. Make the dictionary your friend and it will become a companion to your students also. Children need to see you using the dictionary.

Suggested activities

There are a number of specific activities you can carry on in your classroom to encourage the use of new words as well as to develop word awareness.

1. Password®

The popular television program can be adapted for classroom use. I have scheduled the game once a week and continued it for much of the school year, accumulating the team scores. There are numerous adaptations you can work out, but here is one way.

Divide the class into two teams. Have two members from each team go to the front of the room and sit either at a table or at desks which face the classroom. Give the same word, printed on a card, to one member of each team at the table. The person with the word card is to give his teammate single word clues, and the teammate is to guess the word his partner is holding. Each team takes alternate turns. On the first guess if the word on the card is given correctly, ten points are scored. If it is not given until after the second clue then nine points are scored. For every clue that must be given the score is reduced one point. If the game goes to one point and the word is not guessed, then the word is identified and no score is given. As soon as a word is guessed correctly, the team that did not score replaces its members with two new players.

This game is quite challenging. Children discover how difficult it is to give single word clues, and as time passes they sharpen their ability to use the best clues. They also learn to listen carefully to the clues given by the opposing team because these can be even more useful than those clues given by one's own team. The words used as passwords may be related to specific areas in science or social studies that you are studying or have studied during the year. They also can come from lists submitted by the children, or you can select them from various dictionaries.

2. Scrabble®

This commercial game is available in an edition designed for children. It is also possible to make your own letters for anagrams, a related game. Take strips of lath and cut them into 1-inch pieces. Print a different letter of the alphabet on each piece, including numerous duplicate letter pieces. This game can be played with two to five players. The more players, the more duplicate letters are needed. The letters are all placed face down in the center of the table. Each player begins by drawing five letters. After this each player, in turn, draws one letter. The object is to make as many words (3 letter minimum length, no proper nouns) as possible. The winner is the one with the most words. A dictionary should be handy.

Another related game is the commercial one called Spill-N-Spell.® In this one the letters are marked on the sides of a group of dice. The dice are shaken in a container and then thrown on the table. Only the letters on top of the dice may be used to form words. Scores are made according to number values designated for each letter.

3. Crossword Puzzles

These do not have to be difficult to construct. Do not try to make involved, interlocking puzzles, but rather develop puzzles where either no letters or only a few letters are used for two intersecting words. Your first ones can be words that are written horizontally. Later there can be puzzles with words written only in the vertical position. One variation can be a puzzle with one word provided vertically and clues given for horizontal words, using the letters of the vertical word to begin each puzzle word. An example is Figure 8-1.

Encourage the children to create their own word puzzles. These can be duplicated for others to use.

4. Vocabulary Challenge

I occasionally use one bulletin board for a vocabulary challenge. On the board I place four large cards with a word printed on each. I try to find one word that is likely to be known to all the children, one word that many will know, and two that, hopefully, no one will recognize. The four words are posted for a week. During that time I challenge the children to use each word in a *normal* conversation with me.

Each child receives a 3x5 filing card which has his name at the top. When the child is successful in using any of the posted words in conversation with me I write the word on his card and punch a hole next to the word. A child may get punches for using a word several times during the week. The very first week I make this challenge I am quite lenient, and it is amusing to see a child approach me, grope for words, twist his head repeatedly toward the bulletin board, and finally come up with a sentence using one of the challenge words. After the first week I point out that if I have any hint that a child is trying to use

F									
1									
R									
2									
I									
3									
E									
4									
N									
5									
D									
6									
S									
7									
H									
8									
I									
9									
P									
10									

1. Found in some pillows.
2. An animal with black rings on its tail.
3. A body of land surrounded by water.
4. Country where the pyramids are located.
5. Facial feature.
6. A doe.
7. A shop.
8. Horseback riding equipment.
9. To separate from the group.
10. Gifts.

Figure 8-1

one of the words as he talks with me, then it is not a *normal* conversation and credit cannot be given. It is most rewarding to me when a child has been talking and suddenly says, "Well, don't I get my card punched? I used one of the words," and I realize how truly natural the child has made his conversation. The new vocabulary must really belong to him now.

5. Files

Encourage children to collect new vocabulary words and phrases. These can be kept in personal filing boxes or in a room file. They can also be entered in a notebook or booklet. To be effective there must be opportunities provided for sharing these collections and for using words collected in subsequent writing. Children can organize their files into various categories, i.e., words, phrases, descriptive words, words about feelings or action, more words for "said," etc. Such organization will make the files more functional, and children will turn to them frequently as they develop creative writing pieces.

6. Build Sentences

Take time, at least occasionally, to guide children through an activity which encourages constructing a more interesting sentence. Write on the board, "The boy went to the house." The children then write this at the top of their papers. Ask the children to write the sentence again, adding a word in front of "boy" to describe him. Then have them rewrite the new sentence, this time changing the word "went" to one that gives the reader a clearer picture of how he moved. Write the sentence again, now adding a word to describe "house." Then have the children share their final sentences with each other. Another time you might ask the children to use phrases instead of single words as they build upon a simple sentence. You could suggest an image as an addition. In the sentence about the boy you could suggest an image for describing the manner in which he went to the house. Another time you could have the children replace the nouns.

7. Play with a Long Word

Choose a word such as *leadership, Thanksgiving,* or *consideration.* Challenge the children to make as many words as possible using the letters within the original word. They can make different lists, each one beginnng with one of the letters from the long word.

IN SUMMARY

1. By your own speech set an example of the importance of words. Be alert to new ways of expressing ideas. Encourage the use of

new vocabulary by your own use of appropriate words and your genuine interest in children's efforts to use unique expressions.
2. Share excellent literature as a basis of vocabulary awareness and development.
3. Help children make the dictionary a friend.
4. Use bulletin boards, notebooks, duplicated sheets, files to further interest in vocabulary.
5. Provide activities such as games, puzzles, and guided lessons as opportunities for children to build their vocabularies.
6. Be sure there is *frequent* opportunity for children to express themselves. React with genuine interest and sincere curiosity to ideas children produce.

Bibliography

GARRISON, WEBB B., *Why You Say It: The Fascinating Stories Behind Over 700 Everyday Words and Phrases.* New York: Abingdon Press, 1955. A most useful resource for the teacher as it gives brief explanations, or word-histories, under such categories as "lingo of the sea," "games, sports, hunting," "clothing and adornment of the body," and "science, mechanics, invention." Older children would find this an interesting book to browse through if it were available in the classroom.

GLAUS, MARLENE, *From Thoughts to Words.* Champaign: National Council of Teachers of English, 1965. A highly readable and usable book for elementary school teachers with specific activities about poems, games, authors, stories, and word pictures. The middle section of the book entitled "Word Fun" suggests numerous activities to stimulate interest in words.

LAIRD, HELENE and CHARLTON, *The Tree of Language.* Cleveland: World Publishing Company, 1957. This book is designed for use with older elementary school children. It is written in a serious vein but captures the magic of our language and its relationship with other languages. Some of the chapter headings are: "How did language begin?" "The making of an alphabet," "English spelling and how it got that way," and "Odd things about words."

MERRIAM, EVE, *A Gaggle of Geese.* New York: Alfred A. Knopf, 1960. *Small Fry.* New York: Alfred A. Knopf, 1965. Both of these delightful books are meant for the very young child, but I find them useful as well as appealing to all ages. Miss Merriam has created two excellent books that help to extend a child's vocabulary. In *A Gaggle of Geese* words are introduced to be used to name groups of specific animals such as a herd of elephants, a sloth of bears, and a gam of whales. In *Small Fry* children meet the names of baby young such as kitten for baby cats, beavers, and jack rabbits, joey for the baby kangaroo, and small fry for young fish. The text in both books is written in superb style and each is attractively illustrated. There is a need for many more books of this ilk.

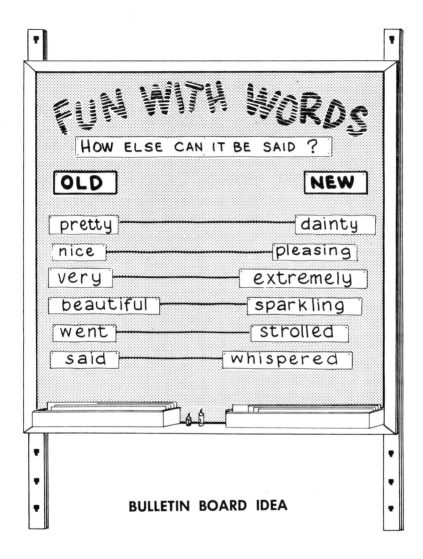

BULLETIN BOARD IDEA

COMMENT: Periodically the old words should be changed. At the base of this board there should be a box of tagboard cards and a felt pen. Both children and teacher could write cards for the new side. There could also be a box where children could place examples of their own writing where they have used new words from this board.

Establishing Clarity in Writing — Experiences and Descriptions

What to write about

As children in our classrooms become fascinated with language through a carefully planned literature program, challenging oral activities, and a constant search for the "best" word, it is most natural for them to want to create their own literature and to give it a permanency that writing offers. Sharing one's thoughts in a written form should be one of the greatest joys of literate man. No other animal can accomplish this feat, and no other species has, through written communication, the power to bring peace, love, and appreciation to its members. The written word is a powerful force for good, and we teachers have a most serious responsibility to inspire the desire of our students to use and share it to the fullest. (How tawdry, in this light, is the thoughtless teacher's "punishment" of requiring certain children to write a 200-word theme or to copy "I will pay attention" 50 times!)

Subject material for writing at all ages is as close as the classroom, the school yard, the neighborhood, and the homes of the children. Writing from personal experiences should become a very natural thing for all of us to do. By helping children sharpen their observational skills and by challenging each writer to write about an experience so vividly that the reader feels he has had that experience, we teachers can do much to put the writing of personal experiences high on the priority list of creative endeavors. The very young are eager to tell about themselves and have their words recorded, but older children often feel that their own lives lack the color and the excitement to which they are accustomed when they encounter the printed page. This may also be due to a tendency on our part to assign such broad topics as what happened over the weekend or during last summer. Some feel there is nothing much to say, while others produce lengthy but dull blow-by-blow accounts of every moment. To improve this situation we need to tighten up our topic assignments, perhaps getting each writer to take one very small part of an experience upon which to elaborate. For example, instead of writing about all the things you might have done over the weekend, choose the shopping trip your family took to a neighboring city on Saturday afternoon. Rather than try to write about the entire trip, choose one aspect such as when you tried on several different coats and had to decide upon one for purchase. Can you get the reader to really feel that he tried on the same coats, used the same dressing room, and felt as you did about your final choice?

In attempting to focus your topic assignments, consider aspects of experiences and descriptions that appeal to certain of the five senses; also consider those aspects that evoke a strong personal feeling, either of pleasure or distaste. Think along with the children in determining the possible "pieces" of an experience that could be selected and written about in more detail. For example, one year when the third graders began a four-day cycle of swimming lessons at the local college pool I divided the first day's experiences into three possible parts: (1) the bus ride to and from the pool, (2) the shower-locker room, and (3) the pool area. Each of these three had been exciting to different children. Every child selected the part he wanted most to write about—the part he felt he could "capture" for his readers, so that they, too, might share his feelings. I could have focused our attention on just the actual swimming experience and made such divisions as: (1) sitting at poolside and receiving instructions, (2) in the water for the swimming lesson, (3) free swim period, and (4) the diving boards. I made my decision as to how to divide the experiences on the basis of my observations of the children, many of whom were more highly stimulated by the bus ride and the college dressing room than they were by the swimming lessons. (The dressing room showers were so fascinating, I nearly had to carry some youngsters out when it was time to leave!) What I am stressing here is that one does not just divide an experience into suitable phases based on an intellectual appraisal, but rather one must consider the specific children and how best to interest them in a writing topic that is right for them.

Setting the conditions for writing

There is one basic purpose we should have when involving children with writing: we want to encourage children to *voluntarily* and *eagerly* turn to writing as a means of effectively expressing themselves. Thus, every time we have boys and girls write we should be able to say afterwards: "Their positive attitude toward, and interest in, writing has been increased." (Again, what justification can there then be for requiring someone to write, "I will be quiet" 50 times?)

Successful writing conditions for children depend upon each child's image of himself. As teachers we are faced with the frightening reality that we contribute to the self-image of each child no matter what we do. Our intent must be that such contributions will be toward developing a more positive self-image within each child and not toward destroying or damaging the view each child has of himself. You and I should end every school day with the question: what did I do today that enhanced some child's concept of himself? And that question has an unfortunate companion, but it, too, must be considered: what did I do today that was detrimental to someone's self-image?

This is not the book to go into this in detail but let me

suggest a few possible ideas. *Genuine* praise, given to *all* students, including those who are "problems"; an effort to remember your own childhood and possibly thus to empathize with the children you are teaching; and a concerted effort to be patient, never yelling, and always showing the kind of respect for *every* child that you would expect to receive yourself—these surely are guides for each of us in striving to contribute to the building of positive self-images within the students we teach. More specifically, the writing program in your room can, itself, do much toward the development of desirable self-concepts, for it should provide a consistent opportunity for each child to look into himself and draw out some impression which then becomes clearer, more precise, in the act of being written down. Moreover, the regular recording of experiences which then are shared by an interested group of classmates and a very receptive teacher adds to the building of better self-images.

How does a writing program get underway? From the first school day in September try to communicate with your students that one's daily experiences are of value, and when written after careful planning even the most common kinds of experience may be of interest to others. You will be conveying this idea when you take time to enjoy visiting with your students, when you ask pertinent questions that reflect your interest, and when you help them develop vivid, articulate ways of writing out their experiences. You may find that in writing some of your own experiences you gain a better appreciation of the struggle that creating with words entails as well as showing by example the possibilities of using common experiences as a basis for writing.

Next, establish a definite period of time (daily, if possible) when your students know they may write. This probably should be about ten minutes long (at least early in the school year), though for many students who become readily engrossed in writing and require a longer time, perhaps you can be flexible enough to permit them more time. But for those who find ten minutes too much you might suggest one of the following:

1. Write anything, even nonsense phrases, without pausing during the ten minutes. This may go on for several days until you

find yourself beginning to write something of consequence.

2. Sit and concentrate on experiences you have had. *Think* out alternative sentences that might express each experience. When you feel ready (pleased with some of your thought-sentences) begin to write them out. It may take a day or two for you to feel ready to write.

3. Read from a library book (or others available in the room) with the purpose of noting how the author has described various experiences effectively in order to get ideas for your own writing.

You may find the third choice is one that some children take refuge in in order to avoid the effort of writing. Any child who chooses to read during this writing period must be reminded as often as necessary that the purpose of reading at this time is to stimulate his own writing.

This regularly scheduled time for writing is a time when your students are *free* to write. It is a separate period from the structured, motivated writing periods which you plan. It is a time when your students will do all sorts of writing, including the keeping of a journal or a long continued story as well as experiments in creating poetry, dramas, and nonfictional material. This chapter and the next three provide numerous ideas for planned writing lessons when you regularly guide your students in the development of their composition skills through providing instruction in various types of writing. As the year progresses many students will also use these learnings during the designated *free* writing times as well, but it will be their choice then, not yours.

To continue, a third element necessary in getting a successful writing program underway is the provision of something in which to write, such as a section in a loose-leaf notebook or a separate spiral notebook for the intermediate children and tablets or plenty of loose paper for the primary children. Folders made of manila paper for each child will serve as a permanent place for the writings of primary students. A notebook or folder gives a desirable status to creative efforts and the act of writting. It also provides a sequential collection of a student's writing endeavors, which is particularly effective when he discovers with the turning of the pages an improvement in his ability to express ideas on paper since the beginning of the school year.

Finally, you must be alert to subject matter for writing topics based on experiences. This means that you will plan actual experiences such as field trips, films, readings from children's literature, resource people who come into the classroom, and manipulative experiences. Your alertness will be evident as you take time to talk together with your students about current events both on the national and world level as well as on the local scene. Such discussions should emphasize interest in vocabulary growth and encourage personal reactions.

Suggestions for specific topic assignments

Planned writing experiences need to occur *at least* twice every week, all year long. The best programs will have such experiences happening four times each week with the fifth day set aside for finishing touches.

In the primary grades and kindergarten the program will depend largely upon dictation by the children, and the actual handwriting will be done by the teacher or by boys and girls from the intermediate grades who are scheduled (or invited on the spur of the moment) to come in and take dictation from individual children. If the older children provide the handwriting, then over a period of days or weeks the finished products should usually result in small booklets. When the teacher acts as scribe for group dictation the result will be a collection of chart stories as well as chalkboard stories which the children then copy on individual sheets of paper (though this type of copying can quickly be overdone), or the teacher may type on duplicator masters and thus end with printed booklets of class stories for each child to read and take home.

At either the primary or intermediate grade level the topics for writing are similar. Familiar experiences serve as one of the best starting places, and they are useful throughout the year. Writing about a current pet, or a pet one would like to have, or a pet one had once (these three choices should be able to involve an entire class in writing on the subject of pets) is often a favorite topic, for the children usually feel quite close to animals. When your students write about pets stress the need to tell enough so the reader feels he knows the pet, too. Sometimes when a student writes something like this: "I have a pet. It is a dog. It is lots of fun," I tease the child with such comments as, "I like this piece you wrote about your weiner dog and the way you get it to chase its tail." That comment is almost sure to get a look of surprise as a response and then something like, "I don't have a weiner dog. It's a great big shaggy Irish setter and it doesn't chase its tail, but it does love to swim out to get a stick when I throw it into the pond." Then I point out that what the child first wrote left too much to the reader's imagination and that what he was saying to me would help the reader if it were written down.

Here are several examples of writing about pets by third graders who had been reminded to tell enough so the reader would really be able to picture the pets:

> I have a kitten. It has white paws. Her name is Slippers. It is gray and white. I have a dog, too. It will have babies in December.
>
> *—Steve O.*

> I am going to get a dog. I am going to name him Henry. I am going to get him for Christmas. I am going to train him to catch sticks and bones.
>
> *—Gary G.*

> I was riding bareback on Colonel Blaze and I was galloping. I went around a corner and stopped suddenly! I fell off to the side! I landed on a clump of grass and it still hurts.
>
> *—Kelley R.*

Besides ideas about pets, other pieces on animals can be developed. Older children might tell about the raising and breeding of horses or beef stock after visiting a farm or reading about such animals. A trip to the zoo (or a film) could evoke writing. A student should not write about an entire trip but should select one group of animals or an individual within a group to describe. Another way to stimulate writing about animals is to bring them into the classroom. We once had an all-afternoon visit from a beautiful Siamese cat who felt content to wander over the bookshelves, sit on different desks, wash himself, and go from child to child begging to be petted. That visit brought forth many vivid written descriptions, some poetry, imaginative stories, and numerous illustrations. Another visit that stimulated some imaginative writing was when a third-grade boy brought a great white goose to our class. Fortunately it spent the day in a special pet cage with wheels, for it was very loud and equally noisy and there were times when we pushed it into another room. Here are a few samples of the children's efforts:

> Today Kelley brought a goose. The goose hissed at me. The goose was big. That goose was funny.
>
> —*Craig J.*

> Kelley brought a goose to school. The goose made funny noises. The goose hissed at me. I was scared! The goose scared the children, too.
>
> —*Jeff B.*

Children do not always have to stick to the facts, for it is fun to introduce a little fiction into a real event:

> There was a goose and I stuck my finger in the cage, and the goose bit it off.
>
> —*Anna F.*

And then some children take the actual presence of an animal as the basis for a complete but amusing fiction:

> Once upon a time there was a goose. But this goose was different than other geese. This goose was a super goose. One day the farmer said, "I am going to kill some geese."

He caught the super goose. The goose bit the farmer. The farmer gave up.

—Andy H.

Once there was a fat goose and his name was Fatty. He ate all day. He was so fat that he couldn't even walk. And one day he fell into a well. He stayed there until his days were over.

—Donny E.

Trips are quite useful as sources for writing. Children should be encouraged to write about trips they may take with their parents during vacations and over the weekends. The emphasis should be on some experience *within* the broader context of the trip. In this way each writer will avoid a monotonous diary-like account and will produce a fuller, more imaginative description. For example, a weekend trip to the countryside in autumn might have in it an hour's walk collecting fall leaves or a shopping spree at a roadside vegetable stand; a vacation to the beach could include an afternoon of fishing from a row boat or an evening campfire.

There are trips your class can take together, such as a walk to the school's boiler room, across the playground, around the block, and even into the neighborhood. I call these observation walks, and when we go on one we know that we are looking for writing ideas. In fact, we take along pencil, paper, and lap boards (quarter inch plywood cut 12″ x 15″ with the edges sanded) so that we can jot ideas down as we go along. Sometimes when we come to a vacant lot or the lawn which belongs to the family of one of the students, we scatter, sit down, and spend ten or fifteen minutes writing. Such walks are appropriate any time, but they are especially effective in the fall when we can plunge into great piles of leaves and respond to the crackling sounds and the bright colors, or in the winter after a fresh snowfall, or in the spring when plants and trees are budding and the first bright flowers are beginning to bloom. I have even been out on a gloomy day when a rainshower forced us to take shelter under a foot bridge in the park where we spent ten minutes writing about the rain.

Here are several examples of writing done by children who either took a walk or found their ideas from looking out the window on a winter day:

Outside it's a cold and frozen world. When you look out you see nothing but snow. So silent and peaceful, nothing moving about. Children are looking out of the windows at the white, still snow. Then the wind begins to blow, tossing the snow around the trees and houses. The wind dies down and the sun lies behind the hills. Now once more the snow is lazy and peaceful.

—*Chris F.*　　Grade 6

As you open the door a cold gust of wind grasps you. You pull your coat tight around you. As you walk along the sidewalk the snow crunches under your feet and sends weird shrills up your spine. Then you feel the cold nipping at your ears. Some snow falls off a branch and looks like a tiny avalanche. Then you hear a yell and duck just as a snowball goes whizzing over your head.

—*Greg M.*　　Grade 6

The icicles are hanging from the street lights. The snow in some places is stained brown with dirt, and in some places is as white as white can be. Footprints in the snow, little footprints and big footprints. Cat footprints and dog footprints. And even in some places bird footprints. The trees are white with snow. The bushes look just like the trees only smaller.

—*Mark M.*　　Grade 4

The trees look like big pieces of coral with the snow lining them, and of course, the icicles are gripping the lights that make them shine at night.

—*Alicia F.*　　Grade 4

If your students go on school camp outings, you have another excellent source for more writing. At camp there should be time for observation walks (I take the lap boards along), and you should pause long enough for children to compose brief written thoughts. The following was written by a fifth grader at camp during a walk when we stopped halfway up a rocky hill and turned around, sat down, and looked out over the countryside:

> Each tree can only be a work of God. Each green of a pine an individual blend of nature. Nature is immense in all its natural beauty. Man is not capable of such a thing as nature; though his creations are beautiful and range from majestic shopping centers to green artificial trees. No, this isn't nature. It couldn't be nature.
>
> Once there was time and room for nature but that is something of the past for some and perhaps for most but not for me.
>
> Now I have discovered true nature, the real thing is before me.
>
> —*Becky S.*

Family and friends should provide subject matter for many more pieces of writing. Children can describe members of their family. They can relate experiences they hear from their grandparents. Telling about a friend they once had when they were younger is possible. When children write about people they should strive for accurate physical descriptions, but they can also attempt to make comparisons, thus creating their first simple metaphors and similes.

Another source would be to appeal to the various senses. Sounds are especially effective. Children may even coin their own sound-words which will add flavor to the writing. Most of the preceding ideas can also lend themselves to composition that emphasizes the senses. A walk on an autumn day is perfect for either sounds of dry leaves being kicked or bright colors catching the eye. Pets make all sorts of noises, and they might also suggest ideas related to textures. Trips, too, can suggest writing that depends upon the senses.

Here are two examples of writing that reflect an effort to include references to some of the senses:

I love to hear the snow crunch. It's the best sound God ever made, or ever will make. It crunches when I step in it, and when cars or sleds go whizzing over it. It tingles my toes.

—*Charlotte S.* GRADE 4

As the car rumbles along, blotches of shimmering water flash through the places where trees haven't sprouted. Other cars shriek by in a distorted blur. Nerve numbing sounds like the loose door handle that clunks every time the car goes over a bump makes you want to get out and walk. When the seat gets sweaty and the seatbelt is too tight to move it makes the trip almost unbearable.

—*John H.* GRADE 6

The teacher's role: to provide motivation and encouragement

In the preceding section something has already been said about the teacher motivating interest in writing by arranging for walks and other field trips. More often your efforts to stir up interest in writing will be within the confines of your own classroom. Regularly engage in conversations that bring out various experiences the children have had. As a conversation progresses you will want to note particular vocabulary that might be useful for all when they begin to write. For example, as you and the class talk about the season's first exciting snowfall that occurred over the weekend you can make a list of common words you hear during the conversation, such as *snowslide, toboggan, shovel, chains, hot chocolate*. This variety of words may help to spur other children as they think about what they want to write.

Monday is perhaps the best day to encourage talk about experiences that happened over the weekend. Occasionally you can get the discussion going by sharing one of your own weekend experiences (and if later you try to write about it just as the children are doing, you will begin to understand what problems a writer faces when he tries to express himself. Most writing assignments we teachers ask of our students we should also do.).

As you read selections of good children's literature, be on the lookout for passages to share with your students as examples of fine descriptive writing. Such a selection as the following from James Houston's *The White Archer* might be projected via an opaque projector and the author's use of language noted: [1]

> The long white Arctic spring faded as the sun of summer wheeled above the island. Everywhere the soft gray tundra moss appeared through the snow, and the tiny Arctic flowers unfolded like colored stars. Small birds returned from warm lands in the south and sang their songs as they hopped about gathering dried moss for their nests. The weather softened, and warm mists rose in the early morning. It was a joy to hear the faint bird sounds after the long silence of winter, for it was as though the whole world were being born again. The sun never left the sky.

In this particular passage one might point out the effective choice of verbs: "spring *faded*," "sun . . . . *wheeled* above," "flowers *unfolded*." Or you might focus on descriptive phrases: "warm mists," "faint bird sounds," and "long silence of winter."

Another way to stimulate interest in writing topics is to share the work of children from previous years. Collections of such writings could be placed on the library shelf for browsing. You can also read aloud samples from other students as you try to help children improve some aspects of their compositions.

Once the children begin to write it is essential that you circulate around the room (this is *not* the time to retreat to your desk to check other papers or prepare some other lesson!), for you should be available to offer more suggestions to students you discover have not begun to write. These children need your individual attention for further motivation, and when most of the class is writing you are free to offer such help. As you move from child to child you need to be flexible enough to

---

[1] James Houston, *The White Archer: an Eskimo Legend* (New York: Harcourt, Brace & World, Inc., 1967).

alter the assignment. For example, after suggesting that the children write about helping their parents do a special household chore, you may find someone who can think of no such experience. In this case you might ask the child to write about helping someone else, perhaps a neighbor. Then, if this does not get the student started, you may need to suggest some other alternative.

What happens to the writing children do?

It must receive recognition—ending in the waste basket or merely being returned to each child are tangible indications that the writing was not worth the effort. I try to print collections of my students' writings frequently throughout the year. There is something exciting about seeing your own work published, and duplicating booklets so that everyone can have a copy is equally thrilling to each author. I find that these booklets are usually taken home and enjoyed by the whole family.

Children's writing can be posted in the classroom and in hall showcases. Two important considerations: (1) keep a record of whose work appears, for *everyone* should get equal exposure; (2) change the posted materials *frequently*—I have visited rooms where writing dated two months earlier is still being displayed. One week should be long enough for everyone to see and read. Make the bulletin board attractive with colorful backgrounds and attention-getting captions. Usually post the work in the children's own handwriting though occasionally you might type some selections. I have used the primer-sized type for copying haiku poetry that I wanted to display.

Each year you could make a large class book, the size of large sheets of construction paper (12" x 18"). Each child could periodically select one of his best pieces to contribute. These would be pasted onto different colored pages and children could decorate the borders with crayon or crayon-resist. After several years you would have quite a set of class books that each succeeding class could enjoy browsing through.

Publishing children's creative efforts in a school newspaper or literary magazine is another way to give recognition to the writings. This will be discussed in further detail in Chapter 12.

One other way of posting children's writing is to select choice phrases and copy them in larger manuscript letters and then develop a bulletin board for samples of unique ways of expressing ideas.

Evaluation, not the red pencil

I will never forget a fifth-grade boy who, early in my teaching, always brought up any writing assignment after he had finished and said, "Okay, start marking it up with your red pencil." I soon realized that I was not evaluating his work; I was desecrating it. I am not suggesting that you make no marks on a child's paper, but instead of spending your energy on circling misspellings or marking in needed punctuation, save your marks for comments on the *ideas* in the compositions. In September take the time to react, in writing, to each child's efforts with such detailed comments as: "This is a clever way to express your feelings," and "You made such a good start which made me so curious when you stopped. Next time tell me more about the day you_____." By the end of September you will be exhausted writing personal, individual comments on each child's writing, but it should pay off all the rest of the year. After the first month you will be able to make much briefer comments but they will carry more meaning: "I like this"—this comment would have an arrow drawn to a specific phrase. "This was fun to read." "Tell me more." "What happened to_____?"

Some self evaluation can take place when children have opportunities to read their compositions aloud to the rest of the class. Each child should understand that when he reads aloud he may discover errors—words left out or repeated, poor choice of words, inaccurate ideas—but he should feel free to correct himself *as he is reading* because he knows what he wants and we want to hear it that way. Oral reading is an excellent way to improve one's writing. A professional writer told me long ago that everything she wrote had to stand the test of an oral reading.

I hope, as you encourage your children to write, that your attention is on the ideas and the choices of words to express those ideas. The quickest way to kill creative expression is to give your concern only to improper spelling, poor handwriting, and incorrect grammar. A child must have *something to say* and *want to say it* before he can become worried about the tools for saying it properly. Evaluation of children's writing must be in terms of its success in communicating. When errors in grammar and spelling interfere with communication, then, and only then, should one evaluate the writing in the light of these mechanical aspects. Further discussion on this topic follows in chapter 13.

IN SUMMARY

1. Topics for writing are all about us in our daily experiences.
2. The writer's challenge is to recreate an experience as vividly as possible for the reader.
3. An individual should find writing a source of inspiration in the lifelong task of getting to know one's self.
4. The class day must provide time for writing to take place. Writing assignments cannot be left for homework.
5. The teacher must be available during the writing period to offer suggestions and to get those who are stuck going.
6. What children write should receive recognition by being posted and published.
7. Teachers need to evaluate ideas in children's writing more than their skill with such things as grammar, spelling, and handwriting.

BULLETIN BOARD IDEA

COMMENT: Locate pictures from magazines, calendars and advertising brochures that can be used with the above headings, i.e.
(1) Who are you? *(pictures of children showing smiling faces, dirty
smudges, missing teeth)* (2) What have you done? *(pictures of boys
playing ball, girls caring for dolls, a family on vacation)* (3) The
world around you. *(pictures of landscapes, familiar buildings, pas-
toral scenes, etc.)* As children write pieces appropriate to the headings, post them close by. Be sure to change them frequently. Occasionally include your own written efforts.

10

Poetry Writing —
Exercise in Creativity

Build a background with poetry literature

My students know they are free to depart from almost every creative writing assignment I make. In other words, if someone has an idea that he wants to write out, my assignment should be set aside, for the important purpose is that each person has something about which he wants to write. I insist that a child try an assignment only if he has never exposed himself to the kind of writing experience that is being suggested. For instance, a student who always writes mystery stories will eventually hear me say, "This time I want you to try writing a poem. Consider it a challenge." Or if a child writes poetry every time there is a writing period I occasionally will insist that some other form of writing be attempted.

Poetry is a form that few children seem to turn to voluntarily, and this may be due, in part, to teachers who feel frightened about teaching anyone how to write poems. It could also be that children get very little exposure to poetry once they graduate from nursery rhymes. This chapter is intended to help alleviate some of the fears teachers may have. Surely the best starting place is to present poetry to children as an integral part of the year's literature program. This means frequently selecting appropriate poems to read aloud. Children should hear ballads and other poems that tell stories. They should become acquainted with free verse such as that written by Sandburg and Whitman. They should know poems that reflect man's hopes, delights, fears, and doubts. And students should hear enough poetry written by the past great poets and the excellent contemporary poets to be able to recognize such names as Christina Rosetti, William Shakespeare, Henry Longfellow, Robert Louis Stevenson, David McCord, John Ciardi, and Eve Merriam.

Whatever grade level you may teach, include in your daily or weekly schedule time for sharing poetry. Choose an appropriate time and setting, one that your students will expect and look forward to. If possible you might have your students gather near an attractively arranged poetry corner, or to set the mood you might dim the lights and read to them in a partially darkened room. Use poems that appeal to you, for your personal pleasure in them will quickly be discerned by your students. Spend some time practicing reading poetry aloud and, if possible, listen to yourself on a tape recorder.

In addition to poetry by recognized poets be sure to include poems written by children. Richard Lewis' beautiful collection of poems by English-speaking children around the world, *Miracles*,[1] is a must for your poetry corner.

Select poems with the boys in mind, too

I wonder whether the dislike for, or disinterest in, poetry observable among many young men can be traced back to early school experiences with teachers who seemed to have had an insatiable love for sharing poems about goodness, prettiness, fairies, and elves with their young charges. In my teaching I have surprised many young boys by reading aloud such rousing poems as "Casey at the Bat" and "The Cremation of Sam Mc-Gee." Their reactions were so enthusiastic that I wondered

---

[1] Richard Lewis, compiler, *Miracles, Poems by Children of the English-Speaking World* (New York: Simon & Schuster, 1966).

whether they had ever been treated to anything but "sweet" poetry before. This is not to say that rough and tough poetry is the only kind for boys. Far from it. Look at collections by John Ciardi, Harry Behn, and such poems as "Solitude" and "Mr. Zoo" by Eve Merriam for vigorous poetic treatments of subjects such as animals, nature, and beauty. Even politeness, the bane of poetry for many teachers, has been treated with humor and good sense by Martin Gardner in his collection of poems entitled *Never Make Fun of a Turtle, My Son.*

Watch out for rhymes

Too much emphasis on rhyming often results in original verse by children that contains no concern for an idea but rather indicates a desperate attempt to think of as many words that rhyme as possible. If we stress poetry as a very special way of saying something, a way that uses the fewest words to express the largest feelings: loneliness, joy, excitement, worry, fear— then rhyming becomes secondary. Read from Sandburg and Whitman and you will reveal to children the power of non-rhyming poetry. It is very difficult to find free verse for children, but occasionally even a few lines you run across in *New Yorker* or *Saturday Review* will be appropriate for your students. Russell Hoban includes several free verse poems in his recent book *The Pedaling Man and Other Poems.*[2] Here is one:

WHAT THE WIND SAID

"Far away is where I've come from," said the wind.
"Guess what I've brought you."
  "What?" I asked.
"Shadows dancing on a brown road by an old
Stone fence," the wind said. "Do you like that?"
  "Yes," I said. "What else?"
"Daisies nodding, and the drone of one small airplane
In a sleepy sky," the wind continued.

---

[2] Russell Hoban, *The Pedaling Man and Other Poems* (New York: W. W. Norton & Company, Inc., 1968).

"I like the airplane, and the daisies too," I said.
"What else?"
"That's not enough?" the wind complained.
"No," I said. "I want the song that you were singing.
Give me that."
"That's mine," the wind said. "Find your own." And left.

Whenever a student writes a poem and brings it to you for comment, do not hesitate to point out lines where rhyme seems to have taken precedence over idea. If the child feels he has exhausted the possibilities of suitable words that fit his rhyming pattern, then suggest he either set the poem aside and come back to it another day or give up his rhyming pattern at this point and simply concern himself with expressing the idea he has in mind.

Ways to help children write poetry

The observation walk which was mentioned in the preceding chapter is one of the best ways to inspire poems. That autumn day when the leaves are falling all over the neighborhood, that crisp day in January when a gentle snow has covered everything, and that blustery March afternoon when the wind seems to push you down the walk—these and many other days are ideal for an outdoor walk to find ideas for new poems.

Where I live we occasionally get a few days of fog. It is usually a surprise, for we consider fog something that comes to our friends on the other side of the mountains and not to us. But it does come once in a while, though very briefly, to our valley. One wintry noon as I left the school building on an errand I stepped out into a play yard deep in snow. To my surprise there was a thin fog all about accenting the frosty shrubs and trees. This was too beautiful for the children, who were having indoor recess in the gyms, to miss, so when classes resumed after lunch I began by reading Sandburg's "Fog." Then I told the boys and girls of my errand and how I wanted everyone to share what I had seen. We all got our winter wraps on and then walked single file through deep drifts of snow, pausing at times to look and feel and hear this foggy, winter day. As soon as we returned to the classroom pencils and paper came out as if automatically, for I did not need to suggest that we write after this walk. Here are some of the results:

The fog drifts in like a ghost,
It is doomed to wander.
The fog drifts in like a ship
That sails the sky.

—Brian B.

Fog is a misty creature.
Fog is like a velvet blanket on land and sea.
Fog lifts like a bird,
And comes down to make a nest.

—Neil W.

The fog smells delicate but looks
Like dungeon steam.
The crispy edges of ice sound like
A person munching fritos.

—Scott R.

Fog is like a rabbit,
It hops to my door in the still of night,
It licks my hot face with its rough tongue,
Then it quietly sits in my lap and goes to sleep.

—Lorna R.

Both Mark and Jeannette wrote something that *looked* like prose, but they caught a poetic quality which was pointed out when the writings of the class were shared with the entire group. When I printed Mark's I tried to arrange it in the form of a poem in order to show him the potential of his idea.

The fog came rolling by
Telling us not to stay in;
Come out and play in me;
Run by the squiggly path
Or whatever you may have;

Run and play in the crunchy mist;
Have fun with Old Man Winter;
Say when you are through,
If the old tattered windswept fog comes another day,
I'll be out to play!

—Mark K.

Fog gives a bright sting in your eyes. Also it gives you a
chill down your back. If you live out of town it gives you a
feeling of loneliness.

—Jeannette V.

Most observation walks are so stimulating in themselves that
it is unnecessary and unwise to do any more than suggest that
time be spent trying to capture, via writing, some of the sights
or feelings one had. But on those other days when you must
remain indoors, your subject matter for possible poems will have
to come from such things as the present season, a forthcoming
holiday, topics being studied in science and social studies, or
ideas arising from class conversations. Here are several ways to
structure poems that will interest children in their early attempts
to write. One is the cinquain (*pronounced* sin-KANE). There
are several variations and during the year you will want to try
them all. A cinquain has five lines. The first time you introduce
this form you might suggest that the children think of ideas
appropriate to the current season. When a student has thought
his idea through carefully, ask him to attempt to express it in
the following pattern:

> 1st line—one word
> 2nd line—two words
> 3rd line—three words
> 4th line—four words
> 5th line—one word, again.

For example:

> Walking
> Blue skies
> Fresh cool breezes
> New life all around
> Springtime.

A second variation of the cinquain is to use the following pattern:

> 1st line—5 words
> 2nd line—4 words
> 3rd line—3 words
> 4th line—2 words
> 5th line—1 word

This pattern has been successful particularly in the autumn. The pattern seems to lend itself to the idea of leaves falling down. Here are several examples:

> In the fall leaves float
> Down from every tree
> To cover the
> Ground with
> Color.
>
> —*Doug M.*

> Leaves pattering on the street
> Blowing and rolling around
> Your feet. Pattering,
> Pittering, pittering,
> Pattering.
>
> —*Kevin B.*

Kevin's repeated use of two words is all right occasionally, but when a child resorts to this tactic often, I think he should be encouraged to think of other words. Repetition may be an easy way of adjusting to the cinquain pattern, but we need to help students explore more fitting ways to express an idea.

Eventually you will want to challenge your class with the most common cinquain pattern. It is as follows:

> 1st line—one word, expressing title
> 2nd line—two words, describing title
> 3rd line—three words, expressing action
> 4th line—four words, expressing feeling
> 5th line—a synonym for title

You may find that the first time you introduce this pattern there is merit in doing it as a large group. The fourth line is the most difficult and you may get best results by asking, "How do you feel about the subject?" Here are a few examples of this pattern:

> Rabbits
> Furry animals,
> Jumping, nibbling, hopping.
> Adorable soft fluffy things,
> Bunnies.
>
> —*Greg M.*   GRADE 6

> Cookout
> Bright fire,
> Eating, cooking, singing.
> A task full of fun.
> Campfire.
>
> —*Charlotte S.*   GRADE 4

> Hiking
> Wilderness stroll.
> Climbing, jumping, walking.
> Danger, excitement, sore feet,
> Accomplishment.
>
> —*John H.*   GRADE 6

Another variation which is probably the original form of the cinquain is based on a syllable pattern:

> 1st line—2 syllables
> 2nd line—4 syllables
> 3rd line—6 syllables
> 4th line—8 syllables
> 5th line—2 syllables

This variation is best introduced after children have had considerable practice with *haiku* poetry.

Haiku is an ancient form of Japanese poetry. A haiku poem is three lines long with the first and third lines each containing five syllables and the second having seven syllables. Usually a haiku poem reflects an observation made at a particular moment. Its structure helps to limit the writer to one main thought. Most Japanese haiku deal with nature in some way. They call attention usually to an ordinary scene or to a universal feeling. Here are some samples of haiku written by intermediate-grade children:

> Here it comes, the wind
> Blowing the leaves all around.
> There it goes, the wind.
>
> *—Charlotte S.*   GRADE 4

> Cherry blossoms bloom,
> Softly they will speak of spring,
> Oh, why must they fall?
>
> *—Karen P.*   GRADE 6

> Little green leaves push
> Up through the rocky, hard ground
> To find a new life.
>
> *—Larry B.*   GRADE 6

> In melted snow we
> Find cricket that died in shame.
> Shame for not thinking.
>
> *—John H.*   GRADE 6

> Beautiful flowers
> Waking up in my garden,
> The rest will wake soon.
>
> *—Lisa G.*   GRADE 4

> Pink apple blossoms
> Soon shall be red ripe apples,
> Summer ends, we eat. . . .
>
> *—Jessie B.*   GRADE 6

> The frog is croaking,
> The fly is nearer at last,
> Snap! A full tummy.
>
> *—Mike P.*   GRADE 5

Sometimes I wonder
If you like me for myself
Or just my sweetness.

—*Mark M.*   GRADE 5

Haiku is especially useful with children who are easily discouraged with writing. It is a brief form of poetry. There is no need to struggle for rhymes. Each haiku poem expresses a single idea, and thus almost any observation or everyday experience can become the subject matter.

In writing both the haiku and the cinquains you need to emphasize the need to make the best possible choices of words. It is vital in such brief poems not to waste any valuable space with weak fuel. For example, "nice" and "fun" are two words I find students often using. These are words that do not conjure up any vivid mental images and so they are wasted. Also "the," "a," "is," "to," and other similar words should be avoided. Look at the following cinquain:

Spring
Is a
Time to get
Used to the warm
Sun.

This cinquain has only eleven words in which to make an impact on the reader. Eight of the words fail to create any pictures for the mind, and so "spring," "warm," and "sun" must carry the entire load. This is impossible, and so the poem fails.

A few comments regarding the problem of the overused word "nice." Sometimes I write on the chalkboard: "Today is a nice day." Then I ask the students to cite single words that come to mind when they think of a day that is "nice." These single words can be listed on the board and then many of them grouped in pairs of opposites. For instance, "rainy day" is an opposite of "sunny day." A rainy day would be "nice" to someone whose garden is suffering from lack of moisture, and a sunny day is "nice" for those planning a picnic. This activity may help some students realize how empty the word "nice" is.

Once boys and girls get started on creating haiku poems they become fascinated and may spend many extra hours on it. One year I brought my typewriter to school. Then I suggested each child make his own book of haiku poems. I provided 4 x 6 filing cards, a typing eraser, and boxes of colored pencils. The typewriter may have been the prime motivation, but soon we had a very busy group, creating poems (checking them with me for suggestions), signing up to use the typewriter, then doing delightful illustrations on the cards around each poem, and finally binding the whole booklet together with staples and colored tape.

Another way to elicit poetic expressions from your students is to play what I call "first ideas." For example, say the word "orange" and ask everyone to remember the first image that came to his mind after the word was spoken. Then go along the rows and have each child tell what his image was. Either write them on the chalkboard or use a small portable tape recorder. Here are the thoughts of eight people:

> I see a piece of burlap.
> I see an orange, a fruit.
> I see the sun going down.
> I see pumpkins and autumn leaves.
> I see a page in a book.
> I see a candle flame.
> I see a pillow, soft and plush.
> I don't know.

After looking at the lines above one of the eight people said, "Why, it's a poem." Yes, it is. Another time you might play "first ideas" by asking children in turn to respond with the first ideas that are suggested to them by words you give them for a color, an object, and a place. Repeat this sequence of words for colors, objects and places until you have called on all the children. The written result will be a free verse poem with a structure that contains a thought about a certain color in the first line, a certain object in the second, a certain place in the third, and then starts over with a thought about a different color in the fourth line, a different object in the fifth, and so on.

One poetry unit is not enough

When I first started teaching I found that English textbooks always seemed to have a poetry unit tucked neatly into the back pages of the book, and many of my teacher acquaintances found it easy never to get that far during the year. ("Besides, it couldn't really be very important because it's way at the end.") And those who reached the poetry unit did so late in the spring, and it was a hectic scramble to give it a cursory study before plunging into the year's review of the "important" parts of the English text. Fortunately the more recent texts are improving. They still have a long way to go, but at least some of them include consideration of poetry in several sections of the book. One series begins each chapter with a poem and follows with discussion questions for each one.

Children should hear, read, and write about poetry periodically all year long. Poetry is an essential part of one's growing love affair with words and it cannot be relegated to one single unit of study during the year. There are too many holidays, seasons, and special events that are ideal subject matter for the creating of poems.

During the year time must be taken to note the effects of colors and sounds upon our imaginations. Such effects may easily be the raw material for new poems. Also, children can be encouraged to reflect their feelings of joy and sadness in writing poetry. Above all, I think students should feel free to use poetry as their form of expression even when the teacher has motivated a writing lesson based on experiences or one intended to stimulate the writing of stories of fiction. Poetry seems to have a small following, so we must permit our students to explore it whenever they feel a desire to do so.

IN SUMMARY

1. Read lots of good poetry aloud to your children and encourage them to read poetry by providing books of verse in the classroom.

These are basic experiences for helping boys and girls write poetry.

2. Choose poetry to read aloud that has genuine appeal to your students, not verse you think they ought to hear.
3. Avoid poems that are sentimental.
4. Be on the lookout for poems written in free verse, so that children will learn that poems do not always have to rhyme.
5. Allow children to write poems whenever they feel in the mood, even when you have just made a different assignment.
6. Respond to poetic *ideas* rather than form when evaluating your students' efforts at writing poetry.

Bibliography

WALTER, NINA WILLIS, *Let Them Write Poetry*. New York: Holt, Rinehart and Winston, 1962. A very practical book to foster poetry appreciation through many experiences of writing poetry.

BULLETIN BOARD IDEA

COMMENT: Under the heading, **IDEAS**, display pictures of mountain scenes, seascapes, and thought-provoking symbols such as the national flag, a bookmobile visiting a ghetto area, etc. Under the heading, **FEELINGS**, display pictures of people with obvious feelings such as joy, meditation, worry and surprise. Directly under the heading, **UNIQUE WORDS**, there could be posted lists of words and phrases that teacher and children have found. To the right and left, post copies of poems written by students in the class. On the outer edges of this part of the bulletin board place copies of poems written by established poets.

11

Developing Fiction-Writing Ability

You need a literature background

If children of all ages are exposed to good books at school and at home, they are building a solid foundation for creating their own stories. You can do something about reading aloud to your students, as has been discussed in Chapter 1, but you cannot guarantee that every child also gets such exposure at home. Even so, for years I have made it a practice to send home lists of good, recent books that are appropriate to the children I am teaching. I choose stories I believe the parents will find so interesting that they will want to read them aloud at home. Such a list is useful right at the beginning of the school year, and parents appreciate another list near Christmas. A suggested list is included in Chapter 14.

As we read aloud to our students we should occasionally comment on an author's style and upon the clever ways in which he develops a plot. Sometimes we can boil the plot down to two or three concise sentences and then indicate how much more compelling the actual book is.

Blueprint for a story [1]

When someone writes a story which is a series of incidents, I diagram the story on the chalkboard in order to show that a

---

[1] See *The Instructor* Magazine, March 1967, Leona C. Karr.

good story must be more than a string of happenings. *For example,* look at the following story:

> The girls left school together. They stopped at the corner to visit. Then they crossed the street where they joined some other girls jumping rope. Finally it was late and so each girl went to her own home.

The preceding story would diagram out as a straight line:

x	x	x	x	x
left school	visited at corner	crossed street	jumped rope with others	went home

To add interest the story needs a problem incident, something to change the line of action.

x	x	x
incident	incident	problem incident

Perhaps the problem incident for the above story could occur when the girls cross the street and one girl trips on the curbing and appears to have sprained her ankle. To add even more interest, a complicating incident should take place which increases the problem and keeps the action line rising:

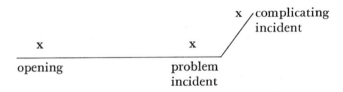

In this story the complicating incident could be when a stranger happens along in his car and offers to take the girls to the nearby hospital. The girls have been warned never to accept rides with strangers, but their classmate is in obvious pain.

The story must continue with possibly other complicating incidents and finally result in a climax, a point where the main character (or characters) solves his own problem or is defeated by it. It is important to help children create solutions to their story problems that are the responsibility of the protagonist. No sudden exterior help should be introduced to solve the problem. Once the climax has been reached there usually is a brief falling action in which all the threads of the story are tied together. The completed story line would look as follows:

After guiding the class through the idea of a blueprint for a story, begin to examine stories from basal readers as well as single chapters from the book you are reading to the class. Finally each child should try to create a story with a problem incident and one or more complicating incidents. The following story is one written by a fourth grader after our first discussion of a story line:

> Bill and Tom were playing by some men who were cutting trees. Suddenly!! A tree fell on Bill's leg. Tom tries to pull it off but it's too heavy. The men cannot hear Bill crying because they are way back in the forest. Tom says he can find help because he saw a house not too far away. Tom runs as fast as he can. Soon he is at the house. He knocks five times then a man comes to the door. Tom tells what happened. The man gets some other men that are in the house. They run over to Bill. They take the log off Bill's leg. And one of the men calls an ambulance. A short while later the ambulance comes and Bill is taken to the hospital.
>
> *—Alan J.*

Such a story as this might be duplicated so that the entire class can study it together. As a class we will determine which sentence serves as the opening of the story. It will be one that attempts to establish the who-what-when-where aspects. Then we will try to identify the sentence which introduces the problem incident, then the sentences that present the complicating incidents, and finally the sentence that contains the climax of the story. Of course, we talk some about who actually solved the problem in the story.

Differentiate between stories and news articles

The youngest children at school should be telling little stories about themselves, about animals, about other people in their lives: the policeman, grocer, fireman, astronaut. And the weaving of stories should continue throughout the school years. An important point to remember is that a distinction ought to be made between fictional stories and informational accounts. It seems easy for primary teachers to call pieces of factual information "stories." Of course, news reporters call many pieces they write stories, but I prefer to differentiate by using the terms "fiction story" and "news story." When young children share an experience, they most likely do it on a straight line pattern. This is suitable for a "news story," but when children understand that a "fiction story" depends upon a story line with rising and falling action they will be more likely to think about possible problems and complicating incidents for the fiction they write.

The dictated story

Until children have learned the basic principles of penmanship and spelling they are unable to create their own stories alone. Boys and girls in the kindergarten and first grade need to have someone serve as scribe to write down the stories they wish to record. Many second graders are ready to tackle their own stories without dictating to someone.

If primary teachers are fortunate enough to have teacher-aids or volunteer mothers, they can have these helpers spend time each day listening to individual children and writing out the stories that are told. If possible the adult helper should use a typewriter. The adult will be able to go faster and thus get to more children if she can type the story as it is dictated. Besides, there is merit in having the child see the words appear on the typewritten page.

If such help is not available, primary teachers might consider "borrowing" children from the intermediate grades to take dictation. Such experiences will serve to provide real language situations for older students—a necessary and welcome change from sterile exercises in an English textbook—as well as provide a setting where older children can have a very humanizing experience with younger children. And these young ones will begin to view the "big kids" as people to respect or emulate rather than fear.

If there are times when a primary teacher can get no one to help take dictation, then it is possible to work out a schedule for the teacher to meet with each child once a week to hear his story. A child could come in a few minutes before school begins in the morning; one or two children might be willing to stay in for a recess (if teacher is willing to forsake some coffee!); several children might be fitted in at the start or end of the noon hour; and if the children have a rest period, several could tell their stories then. There is time if one believes that the very young children need to have opportunities to create stories and then to see them and finally to share them in class and at home.

Once children know there will be regular chances to make up stories they will generally have all sorts of ideas for subjects. Hearing stories by their classmates will stimulate more ideas. You may want to suggest story ideas, particularly the first few times. A few topics to get a class started:

1. A pretend story about yourself.
2. A pretend story about an animal.
3. A pretend story about a special surprise.
4. A pretend story about a special place.

I am using "pretend" here as a word suitable for young children when the teacher wants to encourage fiction. Children will also want to dictate news stories about themselves, their families, and their friends.

Group-composed stories

The group-composed story helps get the class thinking about the elements of a good story. It also provides the common experience of struggling to create an effective idea with words. And finally it encourages a group to work together, to give and take. I preface the first group-story of the year with the caution that this activity will require considerable patience, willingness to change plans, and careful thought.

I introduce the idea of the group-composed story in September. It is a way of getting acquainted, of conveying my love of language to the children, and it helps me spot those who get ideas quickly and those who are much less comfortable working with words. I suggest we create a silly story. We talk about who might be in the story and what might happen. As I sense enthusiasm for certain suggestions offered by different children I begin to write the story on the chalkboard, using the sentences that the children dictate. As the story develops we discover the reason for having to give and take during this activity, for once the story takes a particular direction then many ideas that others have are no longer suitable. For example, if I take one child's sentence about the main character disappearing into a hole in the earth, the ideas of children about the protagonist climbing a tree or being swept up into the air by a giant bird now do not fit, and we must begin to think of what will happen to the character as a result of his disappearing into the ground.

I do not force my will upon the group, nor do I suggest possible directions for a story to take. I try to be sensitive to the feeling of the group in selecting the suggested sentence that many children seem to want. At times we get several alternative ideas and I cannot accurately sense the feeling of the group, so we vote for the idea the majority wishes.

As I write a sentence on the board I often note a cliché or a rather vague term contained in the sentence, and I try to draw from other students more effective words to convey the same idea. It is my hope that students will try to do the same later when writing their own stories.

Though I try not to direct the story in ways that appeal to me, I do point out the need to pace a story so that each problem that is introduced has time for a reasonable solution. Some children suggest complications to a story when it is obviously near an end, so I indicate that such new ideas belong in a new story, or I suggest the students write their own versions of the story, perhaps in chapters so that they can continue with the ideas they have started.

One other control I employ is to remind the class occasionally that resolutions in a story are best when they have been prepared for earlier in the story. In other words, the writer should not reach for solutions just out of nothing, but should refer back to the previous parts of the story for suggestions of elements that become a part of the solution. The following story is a silly one written by a group of third graders. Notice that the rat, who turns out to be the cause of the problem, was introduced early in the story. The children did not think the rat would be anything special when they first included him. That occurred to them as they struggled to solve the lady's problem. Now if the children had suggested as a solution that the lady suddenly discovered she was wearing a magic pin that caused all of her trouble, I would have told them that this was too convenient, that nowhere in the story did we learn about her owning a pin, and that to bring it in at the very end makes a weak finish.

THE MAGIC RAT AND THE BOUNCING LADY

Once upon a time there was an old woman. She lived in an old house in the woods. She lived by herself, and she was fat and jolly. Her name was Miss Haley-Hay. Miss Haley-Hay had some problems.

Miss Haley-Hay slept in a shabby looking bedroom. One night she became very cold. She went out in the woods to get firewood for her fireplace. There was snow on the ground. She shivered as she went to get the wood. When Miss Haley-Hay came back with the wood, she stepped

THE MAGIC RAT AND THE BOUNCING LADY

Written by the Third Grade

College Elementary School

The bouncing lady is going outside. Beverly Bennett

Once there was a woman who lived in the woods. She was making a fire.

Linda Lawson

into the house. She bounced up to the ceiling and back down again. When she landed the floor squeaked, and she dropped all the wood. The wood came down with a great clatter and scared her.

In one of the pieces of the firewood there was a purple rat with a pink tail. He bounced out onto the floor when the firewood fell. Then the rat bounded up on the bread shelf. Miss Haley-Hay got up from the floor to put the firewood away. She started bouncing again. "I'm scared," cried Miss Haley-Hay, "I wish I would stop bouncing."

Miss Haley-Hay began to suspect something. She just knew something was making her bounce. She heard something nibbling on her bread on the shelf. She saw the purple rat with the pink tail. She started to go after the rat. But she started bouncing up and down again.

"Oh, dear," she cried. "I do wish I would stop bouncing!"

While Miss Haley-Hay was bouncing the rat hid behind the couch. Miss Haley-Hay cried, "A purple rat with a pink tail!" And then she stopped bouncing.

She started looking for the rat. When she found the rat behind the couch, she started bouncing again. "That rat must be magic. When I look at him he makes me bounce," Miss Haley-Hay said. Then she called out, "Please leave my house, you purple rat with a pink tail!"

The rat disappeared out of the door. Miss Haley-Hay stopped bouncing. She was very happy.

When we finish a story I try to get seven or eight suggestions for a title, and these are written on the chalkboard. The children try to explain why they think one title is better than another. Then we vote. I find it best to vote for three titles the first time, then we eliminate those that received very few votes and vote again on the remaining ones.

After the story is done the children are eager to draw pictures for it, so they take out their crayons and paper. I insist that each picture include a sentence or two on the reverse side as explanation of where the picture fits into the story. Then when I duplicate the story I use a ballpoint pen to trace over the crayon drawings on duplicator masters, and I type in the sentences of the artists as well as their names. This results in an attractive booklet, one that means a great deal to quite a few

Mrs. Haley-Hay is picking up the wood. Brian Bach

LOOKING FOR A FRIEND

Written by the Third Grade

Jeff Bach	Gary Garris	Kelley Rinehart
Barbara Bintliff	Mike Gaines	Forrest Shafford
Barbara Boice	Andy Howard	Susan Tatum
Mary Bruketta	Craig Jensen	Monte Underwood
Suzy Christianson	Steve Ohlde	Billy Vanderhoof
Louise Davenport	Steve Probasco	Paul Waddington
Donny Eckis	John Rairdan	Kim Yee
Anna Floyd	Eddie Richard	

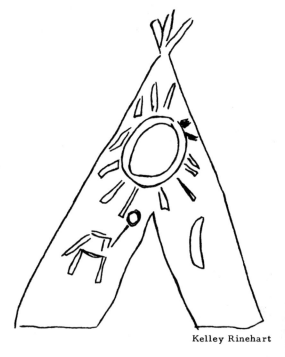

Kelley Rinehart

November 19__
College Elementary School
Ellensburg, Washington

Anna Floyd

LOST IN THE FOREST

Barbara
Boice

A young Pilgrim boy walked toward the Indian village. The boy was lonely. He was going to find a friend. A wild turkey strutted out from some bushes. It frightened the boy. He jumped. He started running. He came to a cliff. He looked down and saw an Indian village.

"Oh, I want to find a friend. I am very lonely," said the Pilgrim boy. The boy looked for a path. He saw a little path that led deep into the forest. He followed the path. His foot tripped on a rock. He fell into the bushes. There in front of him was a friendly fawn. When he got up he saw several paths. He did not know which one to take. He followed one path which just led deeper into the forest. There was a rustle in the leaves, so he stopped. Something wet tickled his hand. When he turned around he saw the fawn.

"Hello. Here's a friend for me." So the two started walking again. It was getting darker. Suddenly the boy realized he was lost!

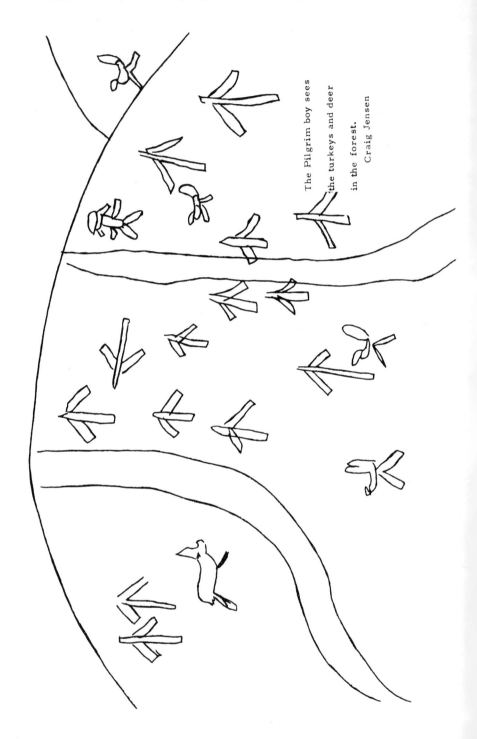

The Pilgrim boy sees
the turkeys and deer
in the forest.
Craig Jensen

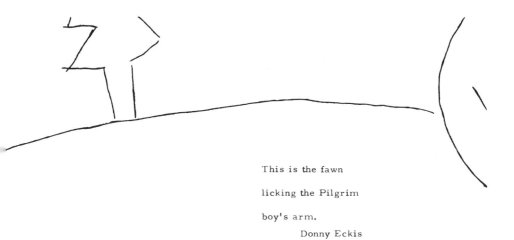

This is the fawn

licking the Pilgrim

boy's arm.

Donny Eckis

A LITTLE LOST FRIEND

Barbara
Bintliff

It was getting quite dark. He tried to find some place to sleep. Finally he got some leaves and made a bed out of them. He got some more leaves to cover him up so he could keep warm. The boy looked around and saw the fawn lying by his side.

"You're the nicest friend I've found yet." said the boy. The fawn started to lick his ear, and the boy fell asleep.

Morning soon came. The boy woke up. He started on the path again with the fawn following. He didn't know he was following an Indian trail. All of a sudden he thought he saw a turkey behind a rock. When he got there it was only a small Indian boy out hunting.

The little Pilgrim boy walked up to the Indian boy. They both were a little scared. The Pilgrim boy was afraid the Indian boy would kill the fawn, but then the Indian boy called, "Here, little Cheeko." The little fawn jumped over to the Indian boy. The Pilgrim boy said, "Is this your little fawn?" The Indian boy said, "Yes, it is."

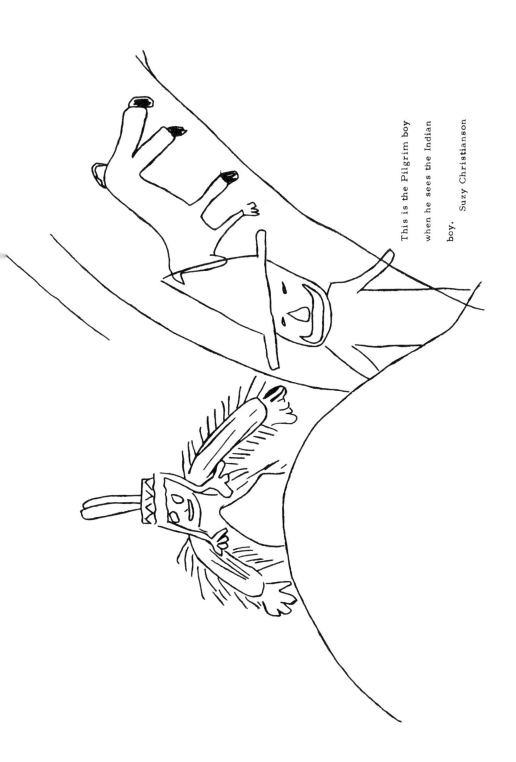

This is the Pilgrim boy when he sees the Indian boy.   Suzy Christianson

The Pilgrim boy suddenly felt sad. He thought he had lost his only friend.

AT THE INDIAN VILLAGE

The Pilgrim boy was sad, but he was hungry, too. He asked the Indian boy, "Is there anything around here I can eat? I am hungry because I haven't had any food since yesterday." The Indian boy asked him why he had not eaten anything since yesterday. The Pilgrim boy said, "I went on a walk yesterday. I wanted to find a friend, and I got lost."

The Indian boy said, "Thank you for finding my fawn. He is my friend. You did something for me. Then I'll do something for you. Follow me." He took the boy back to the Indian village that the Pilgrim boy had seen when he was looking over the cliff.

When they got to the village they saw all the Pilgrim families. The families wanted the Indians to help them find their boy. The Indians said they would help.

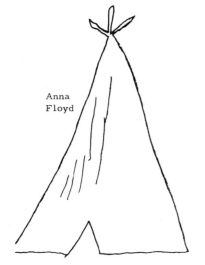

Anna
Floyd

All of a sudden the two boys slid down the hill. Everyone heard the boys laughing. The Pilgrim families ran to the boys.

The Pilgrim boy spoke in an excited voice, "At last I have found a friend. The Indian boy is my best friend."

The Indian boy said, "No, you have two friends."

"Who is the other friend?" asked the Pilgrim boy as he looked around for the other friend.

The Indian boy said, "You have Cheeko and me as your friends."

THE END

Louise Davenport

This is where the Indian boy met the Pilgrim boy, and the Indian boy called the deer to come to him.

Paul Waddington

The Indian boy and the Pilgrim boy are sliding down the hill. The Pilgrim families all looked at them.   Barbara Bintliff

people, for everyone helped create the story and some children contributed the illustrations.

Once each month through December I have the class create a group-composed story, and by the end of the fourth one I am sure that *every* child has had at least an illustration in one of the stories.

Here are examples of stories written for the other three months. In October I ask for a *spooky* story. In November I tell the students that I am going to contribute the first sentence and that I would like them to try to make this a *friendly* story. In this way I avoid too much emphasis on violence which some children are inclined to stress when Halloween or Indians are the subject.

MYSTERY AT GHOST HOLLOW

The witches and black cats were meeting at midnight on the night before Halloween. They were meeting in Ghost Hollow near Skeleton Stream. They were going to choose witches and cats to go haunt people on Halloween. The witches and cats became angry at each other because the cats thought they should go alone, but the witches said they needed the cats to go with them to help cast eerie spells. The head witch cackled in a high squawky voice, "If you don't go with us we will put a spell on you."

The cats meowed in a sneaky way, "Let's see you do it," and walked over to the rheumatism kettle.

The witches gathered in a huddle to plan their spell. The head witch said, "Let's turn the cats into rats." The other witches laughed, "Heeeee, and we can have rat stew!"

The witches called the cats back. The cats were whispering and laughing as they came back.

The head witch went over to a cupboard. She took out some magic ingredients. The witches dumped the ingredients into the kettle. An eerie smoke arose. The witches chanted, "Abra Cadabra Razza Matazz."

All of a sudden there was a big boom. When the smoke cleared the *cats* were licking their chops.

THE MORAL OF THIS STORY: If you are a witch, don't disagree with a cat.

—Written by the Fifth Grade

You will notice that in the long story I was able to include the drawings of more children because I would trace just a tree or tepee from someone's paper and use it in the margin.

The December story is a group-composed story but it is considerably modified. As with the November story I provide the first sentence (I use the same sentence each year), but I tell the class that this story will be more challenging because it will have only as many sentences as there are people in the room. This means that since everyone will contribute only one sentence we have to be very careful to introduce our problems early enough so that good solutions can be made. The first few students I call on *(I arbitrarily follow the seating order)* must set the scene, the middle children must be careful not to solve all the problems or introduce new ones that are too complicated, and the last few children must conclude the story.

When you go in order this way you occasionally come to a child who is very shy or one who has great difficulty suggesting ideas. In such cases I look at the story on the board, and rather than try for a clever move in the story, I simply ask what would happen next. *For instance,* if the story says Santa fell down, I might ask what a person does right after he has fallen down. And the child may answer, "He says ouch," or "He gets up again." Whatever is said I usually accept; I write it on the board and go on to the next child. I prefer not to skip a child and come back later, for that may become an easy way for students to avoid contributing.

SANTA'S BAD NIGHT

It was midnight Christmas Eve. Santa started to fly his sleigh. Santa said, "Hi ho!" All the reindeer had to get out of the sleigh to push because the motor wouldn't start. The reindeer couldn't fly. The motor started suddenly and left Santa behind. Santa didn't know what to do, so he called for help. When help came and they got started again, Santa fell out with a bump. He broke his leg. The motor stopped again and they couldn't get started, so the sleigh and reindeer both fell down. Santa started to get up and his leg fell off! When Santa's leg fell off he flopped on his belly. And

Santa thought he would never be able to walk again. Mrs. Santa saw him and came to help. When the reindeer saw Santa's wife they began to run to her and slipped on the ice. Mrs. Santa put Santa's leg back on. Mrs. Santa helped Santa push the sleigh right side up. Since the motor wouldn't start Santa fixed his sleigh up with wings. He left the reindeer behind and flew to the first house where he fell into the chimney head-first because he slipped on some ice. Then he remembered that he forgot his bag of toys. He wiggled himself around in the chimney but he only moved an inch. Back at the North Pole, Mrs. Santa and the reindeer saw the bag of toys, so they went to give him his toys. They went in his other sleigh. When they saw Santa stuck they tied a rope on his feet and pulled him out. He was so glad to get his toys that he fell off the roof backwards. He landed on his belly, bounced back up on the roof. He said this chimney was too little for him to go down, so he asked Mrs. Santa to take the toys down. So he went on to the next house. Santa went one way and Mrs. Santa went the other way, and they got all the toys to all the houses, and then they went home.

—Fourth Grade

By January it is difficult to motivate another group-composed story. It probably can be done, but by this time the children have had so much experience constructing stories together that they find they have too many divergent ideas and are ready to write their own, individual stories. This is as it should be.

Partner stories

Often students like to work in pairs when creating fiction. This may help when one person is better in penmanship, or it may be a boost for someone who frequently is at a loss for an idea. By working with another person who does not have the same difficulty, a student may discover a rather effective partnership. Occasionally three people can work together successfully. One year I had a boy who spent every noon hour with a friend in the library writing a "book." It took three months and was 40 pages long. The same boy also worked with another friend after school in the library and turned out a second book. The mother of one of the boys typed the duplicator masters and the school provided the paper. When the book was printed it was sold at an annual creative writing and paperback book sale. Some of the money taken in helped to pay for the paper. The rest of the money went for materials to enhance the language arts program throughout the school.

Partner stories are fun and worthwhile, but remember there are children who prefer to write alone, and they should have the chance. As for ideas, usually after working on several group-composed stories and hearing good stories read aloud from books, your students will have little difficulty in deciding what to write about. There are a few general ideas that may be useful:

1. Write legends. Tell how something came to be. If you have studied Alaska, create legends about the northern lights. (Read aloud some real legends as stimulus.) Capitalize upon some special geographic feature of your area for legend material. If your community gets lots of wind, write stories explaining its origin. If your town is near a marsh, explain that through legends. You could develop a fascinating collection of legends for your locale.
2. Write tall tales. (Try some after you have read about Paul Bunyan and Pecos Bill.) Perhaps your students can create a new hero.
3. Provide a social situation that needs solving. *For example:*

   > Tommy Tucker is the best basketball player in the room. He likes to win. He practices everyday after school. One day Bobby Shane joined the boys as they were practicing. Bobby Shane is quiet. He does not play basketball very well. He makes many mistakes. What will happen today? What will Tommy Tucker do?

4. Present a situation that stimulates ideas for creative stories. Here is an example of the way I do this whenever our first snowfall of the year happens to occur during the night. I begin by asking the class when it was that different individuals first knew snow had come—was it from their own bedroom windows or did someone in their family tell them? There is an excitement in the air when snow really blankets the town the first time in the season, and most of the children are eager to share their initial experiences with the snow. Then I read the following poem:

A STORY IN THE SNOW

This morning, as I walked to school
  Across the fluffy snow,
I came upon a bunny's tracks—
  A jumping, zigzag row.
He must have hurried very fast,
  For here and there I saw
Along his jerky, winding trail
  The print of Rover's paw!
I set my lunch pail on the snow
  And stood there very still,
For only Rover's clumsy tracks
  Led down the little hill.
Then suddenly I thought I heard
  A rustling sound close by;
And there within a grassy clump
  Shone Bunny's twinkling eye!

—Pearl Riggs Crouch

I point out how the reader is never told until the very last line that this is a story about Bunny. We learn the story by seeing the footprints in the snow. Then I ask each child to pretend that at his home he was the first to see the snow-covered world, and he saw it very early that morning when he opened the front door. At first it looked as though no one had been out yet, but then two tracks were noticed out in the street. Directly in front of the house were footprints leading from the tracks up to the front porch. Then the footprints turned and went back out to the tracks, and the tracks continued on down the street. Then I challenge the students to explain the story in the snow at their houses. This results in all sorts of stories from those expected ones about the milkman to a secret visitor who tried the front door and then decided to go back to his car and drive to the rear of the house and enter from there.

What to do with the stories after they are written

The group-composed stories should be duplicated and made available to the class. On the day I hand the stories out I use the reading period, and we begin by reading through "our" story silently. Then I suggest that different children try to read it aloud. We work on reading with effective expression. Another day we use the story as a basis for creative dramatizations. The one about the Pilgrim and the Indian usually seems to work well for dramatics. The stories can be illustrated on large sheets of butcher paper, using tempera paint, and then the class can prepare to read the story aloud in other classrooms. As the story is read by a group of readers (perhaps one reader per paragraph), other children enter through the door, one by one, at the appropriate moments, holding the large paintings. By the time the story is finished there will be the parts of a potential mural surrounding the entire class. This activity is especially suited for the Christmas story.

The other group-composed stories can be shared on a rather less grand scale. I often have intermediate children use several reading periods to perfect their oral reading of a story and then go to a primary room to read. The children who have difficulty reading smoothly can contribute by reading the captions for the illustrations that have been duplicated in the booklet.

There should be copies of many stories written by the children to take home to share with parents, and perhaps students from other rooms could purchase copies for a few pennies. If the school has a school newspaper or literary magazine this is an excellent place for children's stories to appear. In the next chapter we will consider the school newspaper.

IN SUMMARY

1. Fiction writing is an outgrowth of reading and hearing good literature.
2. Good fiction follows a story line of rising and falling action.
3. Stories may be written collectively by large groups or in pairs and by individuals.
4. The teacher needs to guide children to be selective in their choices of words and phrases in an effort to create writing that is fresh and vivid.
5. Finished stories must be shared among classmates, throughout the school, and at home.
6. There are related reading, dramatization, and art activities that should accompany the writing of fiction.

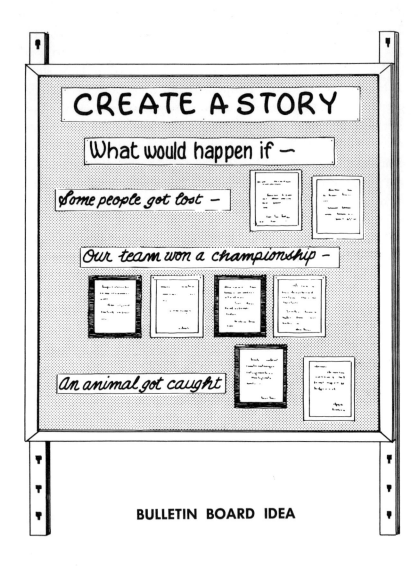

BULLETIN BOARD IDEA

COMMENT: As students write stories appropriate to the headings, post them. Take time to mount the writings on attractive colored backgrounds. Occasionally change the headings. Encourage students to contribute situations for new headings

12

Guidelines to Effective Nonfiction Writing

Writing cannot be divided into "creative" and "practical"

It has been common practice to dichotomize writing into "creative" and "practical," but this easily leads to the faulty reasoning that practical writing is *not* creative. Such a mistake to make! We should be striving for imaginative, fresh ways of expressing ideas *whenever* we write. Practical writing is the name we usually give to the writing of letters, invitations, announcements, and reports, but when involved with such nonfiction writing we must continue to give careful attention to creative expression.

We can demonstrate the fact that the best nonfiction works found in the library are those done in lucid style with writing that is, first of all, accurate, but also well-paced and dynamic in its prose. Some of the work of William Beebe, who wrote scientific material for the layman in the 30's and 40's, contains excellent examples even for today's reader or writer. There are contemporary authors whose work should be examined for its excellent writing: for example, *Masked Prowler, the Story of a Raccoon* [1] and *Vulpes, the Red Fox* [2] by John and Jean

---

[1] John and Jean George, *Masked Prowler, the Story of a Raccoon* (New York: Dutton, 1950).

[2] ———, *Vulpes, the Red Fox* (New York: Dutton, 1948).

George; *Pagoo*[3] and *Minn of the Mississippi*[4] by Holling; the many fine titles in science for young children by Mellicent Selsam; *The Heritage of Music*[5] by Katherine Shippen; and the handsomely illustrated biographies by the d'Aulaires and by James Daugherty.

Writing reports creatively

"Now, class, get to work on your reports. Remember they are to be in your own words, *not copied.*" How many times I have heard this (including the times I have said it), and with some checking I find that, except for this admonition, no planned instruction has been carried out to aid children in becoming able to summarize and paraphrase. When one looks at the topics on which children frequently are asked to do reports, one is not surprised to find that boys and girls copy. What imaginative contributions is a child able to bring to such topics as "Farming in New Mexico," "How a Volcano is Formed," or "Recreation in Holland"? These are topics that are well covered in social studies texts and encyclopedias. So when a child is confronted with such an assignment and finds it as an entry in a book, he would be foolish to rewrite it (and rather likely to do a stiff, colorless job of it, as well).

Topics for reports should stir the imagination and, by their own nature, force the student to use a variety of resources. Such topics take considerable thought to develop because they must be built upon your own particular curriculum. For instance, if your class studies Mexico you might develop this topic: Why is the country's second largest manufacturing city located in an area where the population is 2 people per square mile when Mexico City, the nation's number one manufacturing city, is in an area where the population is 250 people per square mile?

---

[3] Holling C. Holling, *Pagoo,* illustrated by author and Lucille Webster Holling (Boston: Houghton Mifflin Co., 1957).

[4] ——, *Minn of the Mississippi* (Boston: Houghton Mifflin Co., 1951).

[5] Katherine B. Shippen and Anca Seidlova, *The Heritage of Music,* illustrated by Otto Van Eersel (New York: Viking, 1963).

Such a question is not answered in one neat paragraph in a social studies text.

Another example of a topic that would require students to draw upon several sources of information might be: Would Bennington, Vermont be a good place to build a flour mill? There is no correct answer, for one's response depends upon one's argument and accompanying justification. Thus, appropriate topics for reports are those which ask the question "why" or those which draw together several aspects of study and pose a problem for solution.

In order for children to be successful in paraphrasing and summarizing they will need specific instruction. To begin with, your students must learn to take notes. This was briefly discussed in Chapter 5. Your students should understand that note-taking is a way of recording a quantity of information in very few words. It is also a guide for someone who plans to talk on a subject and it is valuable when writing a report.

Simple note-taking can begin with the very young. These children can have experiences listing items such as class duties and daily plans. They can also list the happenings in a story, and here they should try to list them in a logical sequence. Characters in a story can be listed, and they might be listed in chronological order according to initial appearances.

Outlining on a very simple basis ought to begin in fourth grade. Rather than struggle to teach a "correct" form, simply indicate that an outline is a way of arranging notes on a page so that they are easy to read later. The traditional use of Roman numerals is one way. It is also possible merely to use indentations. One of the first experiences a class might have in learning to outline is to take a short field trip, perhaps to the local lumber mill, post office, or fire station. Each child takes a note pad with him in which he has two main sections, one entitled "What I Saw" and the other "What I Learned." This is a start toward learning to organize notes. For example, you will be able to return to the classroom and sort through your pages in "What I Saw" after a trip to the lumber mill, and then these notes can be rearranged into these categories: (1) the lumber yard, (2) inside the cutting mill, (3) at the drying building, and (4) in the retail store. The same categories can then be repeated for the notes on "What I Learned."

Of course, field trips are only one of the types of experience you should provide in your efforts to teach children to take notes. You can supply selections of nonfiction material for the class to work on together in determining the most useful, yet shortest, notes to write down. The reading selection could be projected on the screen and several children could write on the chalkboard the notes suggested through class discussion. Be sure to use a selection related to something the class is studying at the time.

Whenever you show a film, provide several guide questions to aid in the viewing. I try to show a film twice if possible, for I find the students gain much more the second time and are able to jot down better answers to the guide questions. Then we compare our answers. This is not a time for long, detailed sentences. We are looking for the briefest notes that are still able to communicate.

I also prepare brief talks (maximum time five minutes), and ask the children to keep notes of what I say. Afterwards I may hand out duplicated copies of the notes I used for the talk, and we compare my notes with those the children made. At first they find it quite difficult to keep up with someone who is talking, but as they see my very brief notes and we talk about the idea of jotting down phrases or only single words, they begin to find there is enough time, and with practice their note-taking skill improves.

Using our notes, we begin to practice writing complete sentences and paragraphs that are suggested by the notes. So we experience breaking information up into small pieces and later putting it together into acceptable prose.

Writing a book—what it takes to do "research"

If you have access to a local author you can motivate a class, or some members of the class, to write a book by asking the author to visit. An author can say much to demonstrate that his research goes beyond finding information in a single encyclopedia entry. For those who cannot locate an author near by, there is an excellent film that can be substituted. It is "Story of a Book" by Churchill films. In this short film (ten minutes) Holling C. Holling tells how he wrote *Pagoo*. When picturing the research he and his wife did, the camera shows them reading from a stack of different-sized books, visiting a real tide pool on the Eastern seacoast, and finally creating their own tide pool in an aquarium as a way to study the life of the hermit crab who becomes Pagoo in the book. The film also depicts the author-illustrator developing the pictures to go along with the text, and then in the most valuable few seconds of the film Mr. Holling is shown proofreading his manuscript. He is not concentrating on punctuation or spelling, but rather he is striving for more vivid words to express the meaning he wishes to convey. The viewer watches him cross out a dull word and replace it with a very descriptive term. Thus, this film shows how a book is written, tells what research can consist of, and brings out the author's concern for effective writing.

This film is a great motivator for getting children to write their first books. If students come to you with ideas for original books, encourage them by your genuine interest, by allowing them time to do research (they may need to go someplace outside of the classroom or school to see something or someone—do not limit them only to books as sources), and by meeting with them occasionally to evaluate progress and make helpful suggestions. Concentrate your attention on the accuracy of the information reported and on the quality of the prose.

Jean Fritz has written *George Washington's Breakfast*,[6] in which a young boy's insatiable curiosity over what our first president ate for breakfast leads him to do some extensive research. The book is excellent in describing a child who is not satisfied with the first or second book he discovers in his efforts to do serious study.

---

[6] Jean Fritz, *George Washington's Breakfast,* illustrated by Paul Galdone (New York: Coward-McCann, 1969).

Writing letters, real ones

Letter-writing is a common experience for most of us. For children it needs to be more than the formalized "thank-you" letters which teachers so often insist be written to a class visitor, the principal, or another room for some service. The writing of these letters in the primary grades is quite common, but 35 copies of the same letter are not very exciting to receive. Now, it is right to establish among children the idea that one should express gratitude, and letters of thank-you also provide penmanship practice needed by young writers, but letters need to *say something* and that something should not be just an idea developed by the teacher. If you do not believe every child in your room is able to contribute one original sentence in the letter he is writing, simply ask one child to copy the class-composed letter and let the rest of the students send along drawings to express their personal thoughts. But as soon as possible each child should write his own letter. It may include a copied sentence of thanks (a sentence developed *by the class,* not by the teacher), but it should also show some original thought. This may seem like quite a problem to teachers of primary children, but some of this concern can be alleviated by listing on the chalkboard a number of words the children might need. For example, if your class is writing to thank a group for a creative dramatics program you could list the name of the play, the characters, and the scenes in which the dramatizations occurred. Then let the children create their own letters.

Children should have opportunities to write other letters, too. These should be real letters to be delivered to real people and, hopefully, to be answered. Your students might write to relatives, to children in another school, to a child who is sick or has recently moved away, or to someone within your own school. Be sure to seek out correspondents who can be depended upon to answer. If you have a friend who teaches in another community perhaps you can work up letter exchanges several times during the year. It does not matter if your friend teaches the same grade, for there may be even more challenge when an intermediate-grade class writes to a primary class.

The problem of what to say in a letter is quite important. Too many letters you and I receive are of the variety that begins with, "How are you? I am fine." They go on to say that nothing much has happened. They apologize for the paper and the handwriting, and they end with, "Well, I haven't anything else to say." The truth is, the letter did not say anything except to indicate that the writer was alive. This type of letter is a waste of time, paper, and talent.

Children need models of good letters. One of the most interesting, though demanding, ways is for you to carry on a personal correspondence with each of your students. I have initiated letters to members of the class after several months have elapsed, for by then we have a fair degree of acquaintanceship upon which to build. With a large class my letters must necessarily be brief, but I try to comment on something pertinent to each individual and I try to ask appropriate questions. Sometimes I write about learning problems specific people may have. Other times I restrict my thoughts to their hobbies or social concerns. After my first letter it is up to each individual to keep the correspondence going. Whenever a student writes I answer the letter, and so it continues to be the student's responsibility to maintain this letter-conversation with me. Sometimes the letters continue on into the summer, and then we have to avail ourselves of the United States Post Office. I have a standing agreement with every student: I will always answer any letter written to me. The following letter is one from a boy who was spending the summer in Yellowstone Park because his father was a part-time ranger. The first letters this boy wrote in class the preceding autumn were extremely colorless and flat. This letter represents considerable growth:

Dear Mr. Wilson,

Today our family went fishing on the Yellowstone River. We soon found out that if we were going to catch anything at all we would have to use salmon flies. The fish kept taking our bait. But one fish finally got hooked. My brother and sister came screaming from both sides to see the catch. I asked them to find some grass to lay the fish on. Soon I had the fish cleaned and gutted. But that was the only fish we caught.

The walk to the car was extremely hard because the canyon walls were slippery and muddy because of the rain. People kept falling down in the mud. By the time we reached the car we were wet, muddy and in a bad mood.

Sincerely,

Kent

In an effort to help children sharpen their abilities to write letters that are both fun to write and a pleasure to receive and read, you might share two contrasting letters such as the following:

Letter #1

Dear Uncle Jack,

We just finished our trip. It was lots of fun. We saw lots of interesting things. We bought some souvenirs. Well, I can't think of anything else to say.

Your niece,

Ruth

Letter #2

Dear Uncle Jack,

We have just completed a trip through Yellowstone National Park.

After we entered the park on the south side, we saw a brown bear beside the road. He stood up on his hind legs. Father stopped the car so that we could get a good look at him. I wanted to give him some peanuts, but Father said that we should obey the signs along the road which warned us of danger in feeding the bears.

We left the park over a pass called Sylvan. The view from there was very beautiful. But the sights which I enjoyed most were in Cody outside of the park on the west side. There were real Indians who wore feathers, and there were many articles for sale which the Indians made. Ruth and I bought moccasins to use as house slippers.

When we get back home we will tell you more about what we saw.

Your nephew,

Bill

After reading the letters ask the class which one Uncle Jack probably had more pleasure in reading, and then discuss the reasons for the class choice. Most likely the class will pick Bill's letter, not Ruth's. It is important to discourage an explanation that the second letter is better because it is longer. You could create a very long, dull letter to share (one of the "How are you, I am fine" type), and then challenge the class to create *short,* but *interesting* letters.

Another interesting letter writing experience that I have found successful is one in which children take an imaginary journey as a part of a social studies unit and write letters back home telling about the trip. Generally I disapprove of writing letters that cannot be answered but this activity does seem to have merit.

Keeping journals

A journal can serve as a person's confidante. It is a place where one keeps a record of feelings, impressions, and reactions about people and places and situations. It becomes a container for one's thoughts. When I introduce the idea of a journal I make it clear that this is different from a diary. A diary is mainly a chronicle of dates and happenings, but a journal goes beyond that to include inner feelings. I suggest that all of the students try to make daily entries in a journal for one month. If after that length of time students do not want to continue they should not have to. During that first month I provide two to five minutes several times each day for everyone to write in their journals. I also keep one and sometimes I share ideas I have jotted down, and this often encourages others to share their journal writing. Some of the things I put in a journal are:

1. How I feel this morning and an attempt to explain why.
2. A set of descriptive sentences about something I see in the room or out the window or saw on the way to school.
3. An event in which I was involved and an expression of my reaction to it.
4. An opinion about a current issue.
5. Ideas for possible stories and poems.

During the first month I ask that everyone write *something* when time is provided, even if it is a nonsense repetition of a phrase or sentence. In fact, I suggest that the reluctant journalists write any word, phrase, or sentence over and over until they feel like writing something else. After a few of these sessions ideas of merit begin to focus in the child's mind and soon he is writing with genuine interest.

For fifth- and sixth-grade students *Anne Frank: the Diary of a Young Girl* [7] is a fine model of a journal that is compelling to read.

A school newspaper at any grade

To see one's written efforts in print and available to many readers is a thrill most of us covet. The school newspaper is a most appropriate place for children's writing to appear. A newspaper may be published just for one classroom or for the whole school or even for distribution at home. To be a newspaper it must be published regularly, and the children need to learn that publication deadlines are always present. If you publish a collection of student writing one, two, or three times during a school year, do not call the publication a newspaper. Refer to it as a literary magazine. Newspapers attempt to be more current and they appear on a regular publication basis. A whole-school newspaper should be printed no less frequently than once a month. Better yet, try for every two weeks. One

---

[7] Anne Frank, *Anne Frank: the Diary of a Young Girl,* translated from the Dutch by B. M. Mooyaart-Doubleday (New York: Doubleday, 1952).

year I helped a sixth grade turn out a weekly edition. Actually, the class was divided into two newspaper staffs and each one published on alternate weeks. This meant that a staff had two weeks to prepare an issue, but the student body received a weekly newspaper. If the newspaper is published for just your own classroom, it can be shorter and surely can come out once a week. I know of a first-grade teacher who printed a daily, single-paged newspaper. It was quite an asset to her reading program.

A newspaper has three essential purposes: (1) to provide a suitable place for children's writings to be shared with others; (2) to provide opportunities for children to learn and use such language skills as spelling, news writing, other creative writing, vocabulary development, and proof reading; (3) to provide an instrument that may help to draw all of the students who share the newspaper into a closer relationship where everyone is learning to work together successfully.

A newspaper should include written work from *every* student over a period of time. I am not willing to use the newspaper as a prize only for those who turn in neat, correct work, for I have had many students who needed the recognition of seeing their work in print although *they did not even know this*. If I had insisted upon correctness these particular students would have shrugged and decided that this was not an activity for them. I keep careful records in order to be sure that every student gets into print at least once every four issues. This may mean more guidance on my part to help the reluctant child develop something of which both he and others can be proud.

If you are going to produce a newspaper for the entire school, you may wish to send your students out in pairs to be observing reporters in the other classrooms. I ask my student-reporters to spend a half-hour quietly observing a class in session (of course, I have talked to the teachers about this beforehand), and then to come back and use their notes to write up the articles. After the students and teachers in the school become accustomed to our newspaper, they begin to send word to our classroom: "Could you send reporters to room 210 at

2:30 this afternoon? We are going to be doing some interesting science experiments then."

In addition to the reporters from my room students from other rooms often write up news articles as well as stories and poems for the newspaper, but since one cannot depend upon material arriving from other rooms to complete every issue, I always have reporters seeking news.

The format of the paper is important. It should appear in columns, and every article should have a headline or title. (Usually I have done the typing of stencils, but I know of fifth- and sixth-grade students who have done their own typing.) Do not organize a school paper by grade levels. Students should find news about themselves and their schoolmates throughout an issue, and in the process of hunting for familiar stories they may pause to read stories that otherwise they would never see, particularly if the stories or articles were listed under a different grade level. The newspaper could be divided into the following sections: (1) news, (2) information, (3) stories and poems, (4) cartoons, and (5) editorials. Some schools would find it worthwhile to include a section on sports news.

Here are several examples of news articles written by sixth-grade reporters:

SURPRISES AT SHARING

A park in your backyard, right. A little girl in kindergarten has a park where she can play and have picnics anytime she wants. You see, she lives right next to a park.

There were many surprises in the kindergarten at sharing time, yes, new shoes, picnics, and a family of kittens. Everyone had something to share.

—Pauline M.

THE SCIENCE FAIR WAS HERE

"You can see gun powder under this microscope," says fifth grader Sterling Taylor.

"Look at the coins in this box," said Sharon Huss to a college student. "Buzzz!" A booby trap!

"Look, a heart. A heart of a cow." In one jar a whole heart, and in the other jar a cut up heart. All by Marchiea Anderson from the fifth grade room. The science fair was here!!

—Melissa P.

GATHERING AND STRINGING CHESTNUTS

The children in the first grade brought some chestnuts to school. They had about four hundred chestnuts in all. Most of the children helped gather the nuts. Instead of throwing the nuts away the children are going to string them and use them to put on their Christmas tree.

—Sandy B.

NEW WAYS TO WRITE STORIES

The third graders watched an exciting movie on two mischievous raccoons. There was only one thing different about the movie. Can you guess what? There was no sound. Do you know why? Mrs. Jakubek turned off the sound because after the children saw the film, they were supposed to write a story on what had happened.

—Kathy T.

Here is what one child wrote after complaining that nothing ever happened in one room where she was scheduled to observe, and I challenged her to let her imagination go:

I WONDER

Buzzzzz! The first graders were as busy as bees. Anyway that is what it looked like. But I wonder where their thoughts really were. It was such a beautiful day. Could their thoughts be out there? Or could they be at home with that new puppy? Were they planning what kind of mischief to get into on their way home from school? Maybe they were climbing that tall tree just outside the window. They could have been pretending they were the teacher, telling everyone what to do. Of course, teachers know everything. What do you think they were dreaming about? Or were they dreaming?

—Pauline M.

Sometimes we had a special section in the paper called "Who's Who" and in this the reporters wrote up interviews they had with different children in the school. Here are several examples:

CHUCK GAINES

Chuck Gaines, age eleven, reporting for duty in sixth grade. With a family of seven, one dog, one cat, and one fish, he has fun. Chuck does not like school, but likes to play baseball. Chuck also likes cheeseburgers. With green eyes and brown hair he is a nice looking kid.

—Larry N.

LOUISE DAVENPORT

Horses, cats, and hotdogs. Do you like these things? Seven year old Louise does. Louise was born on September 4, 1952. There are five in her family. She has a sister and a brother. She had a black and white cat named Cupcake, but she died.

—Judy J.

Each time an issue of the newspaper comes out I use it as a basis for a reading lesson. We read through the paper silently, then discuss the best aspects of this issue. We look for suggestions to improve the next issue. I make a special point of praising a newspaper that contains many different student names, for this increases our reading public. I also say that an article with just lists of names of children (such as the helpers for the week in first grade) is not an effective way to include names. We judge the effectiveness of the headlines and of individual sentences within an article. Through such evaluation we become more sensitive to creating a truly imaginative newspaper and one that more and more people are eager to read.

IN SUMMARY

1. Most writing, no matter how practical, needs to be done creatively.
2. Report-writing must be more than producing quantities of handwritten copies of the encyclopedia.

3. Children can learn to take notes.
4. Letters should be written with someone in mind; each someone should answer the letter he receives.
5. A journal can become a very personal place in which one continually experiments with written expression.
6. School newspapers provide an excellent outlet for children's writing, and they can be published at any grade level.

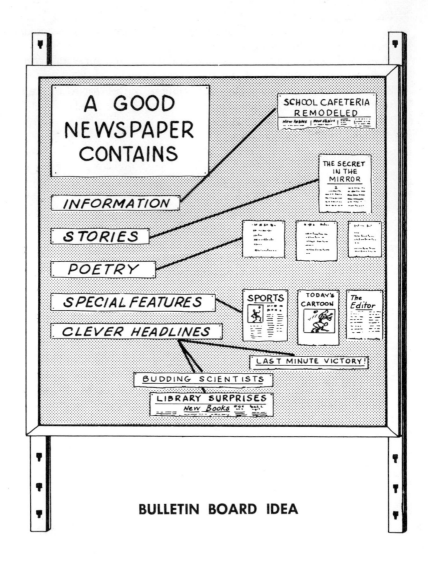

BULLETIN BOARD IDEA

COMMENT: The examples should change each time a new edition of the school newspaper is published. Prior to the first edition this board could exhibit examples from commercial newspapers as a means of stimulating interest in producing a school newspaper.

13

How to Master the Technical Aspects of Writing

The need to have ideas to express comes before skills

Let me repeat what I said in the first chapter on writing: there should be one major objective for the writing program in the schools, which is that each student will *voluntarily* and *eagerly* turn to written communication as an effective means of self-expression. What I am saying is that if we are teaching our students *how* to write then we are successful only if they *do* write.

I am concerned with the fact that many adults look back at English courses in school with distaste. And as one talks with students the evidence of that distaste is found in the high school, the junior high, and the elementary school. When I was in junior high school I remember my best friend complaining bitterly, "What good is English? I don't see why we have to keep taking it every year!" Such a condemnation of the subject which influences our lives every day. Where would we be without our language, and what activities do we engage in that do not depend upon language? When people look back upon English classes as boring or a waste of time, then the teachers of those students have failed. You and I cannot afford to fail to excite our students with the potential of the language and to develop a desire within them to use it as a rich, vivid, powerful vehicle of communication.

It is very likely that this dislike for English grows out of many years of worrying about correct spelling, filling in workbook blanks to show the correct choice between such words as "came" and "come" or "bring" and "brought," writing definitions of declarative, exclamatory, and interrogative sentences, re-copying words that should start with capital letters, or deciding what punctuation marks have been omitted from a group of sentences. This monotonous list, unfortunately, can go on and on for it is about as long as all the combined English assignments some students have had throughout their entire school lives.

The essence of every English class should be the cultivation of and opportunity for expressing ideas. If there are no ideas to discuss, to think about, then who cares about punctuation, spelling, and the other skills? A paper that is neat and correct is wasted paper if the writer has nothing to say, despite the many words that appear on the page. When students discover they do have something to say, that it is important enough to write and to share, then they will be ready and eager to concentrate on the technical skills of writing. Most of our teaching energy should be spent on providing our students with numerous experiences, getting children to write about their thoughts and descriptions, and finally having these students discover the joy of sharing one's written efforts with a receptive teacher and an interested group of classmates. As this becomes the accepted norm of the class, the teacher can begin to help a student improve his written communication by explaining that correct punctuation and spelling can make what one writes easier for the reader to understand.

The problems presented by spelling, punctuation, and grammar

The greatest problem is trying to accept what I have just said, which is: teach skills only when a student expresses his need for them in order to make his writing more comprehensible. I realize that most teachers must abide by school curriculum guides which generally prescribe specific skills to be taught each year. I personally doubt that many students really learn a skill well unless they are ready and see a purpose for it, but I will try to come down from my soapbox and offer a few practical suggestions.

If you must teach prescribed skills then there are some ideas in this chapter to help you. One final caution before going on: if you do not see some definite indications that your students are changing from individuals who have little or nothing to say to individuals who begin, even a little, to want to write, then take time to talk to them and to react to the ideas that do get written.

Spelling

Whenever you have motivated a creative writing lesson, do not let spelling interfere with the flow of written ideas. Tell your students to concentrate all of their attention upon the ideas they are trying to express and then make yourself available whenever someone wants help in spelling a word. Often, just as a writing lesson is getting underway, you and your students can come up with an initial list of words that many will find helpful. For example, if your students are going to write spooky stories in mid-October you might begin with this list: *Halloween, witch, ghost, goblins, mysterious,* and *scary.* The words should be put on the chalkboard, and you should be quite willing to write any others requested by students. By listing them on the board you save yourself the probability of repeating some words over and over; also, as the words appear they may inspire some children who are having difficulty creating an idea. Accept *every* word requested. When children are trying to express ideas, it is not the right time to say, "You should know how to spell that word." The students in my room soon learn that there will be no social disgrace connected with asking how to spell *any* word, including "easy" words such as *is, was,* and *very.* In fact, I find that the more mature students soon find it a comfortable situation in which to get help, too, for they often are more reluctant to admit that they cannot spell certain difficult words needed in their writing than those who ask about simpler words.

If you find yourself tied to the chalkboard listing words when you observe students who need to discuss their problems in developing a written composition, then cease giving help with spelling. Ask your students to try to write words the way they sound and indicate your willingness to help locate spelling errors when you read the papers. Above all, stress the importance of getting one's ideas written down as soon as inspiration hits. Spelling correctness and other aspects of form can come later.

As for teaching children to be accurate spellers, that should happen at another time in the day, not during the writing periods. To be successful with a spelling instruction program it is necessary to help students develop a spelling conscience and a spelling consciousness. This means they will *care* that words are spelled correctly and be *alert* to the proper spelling. The best way to involve your students in such a spelling program is to have each one compete against himself. The traditional five-day sequence of pretest, study, midweek test, study, final test does little to inspire a satisfying spelling program. In fact, it often is deceiving, for a perfect paper on the final test day does not mean one has mastered those words in practical situations. The most satisfactory approach to spelling for me has been the following procedure:

1. Give a list of ten words as a test.
2. Immediately following the test spell out each word, and as

you do so the students should write, preferably in red pencil, each word next to where it was written for the test.

3. Students should quickly survey their success.
4. Now, turn the paper over and give the test to the class again.
5. Once again, have the children write out each word as you spell it aloud following this second test.
6. Ask students to compare the number of correct words on this test with that on the first test.
7. Repeat entire procedure a third time.

This form of test-check-test allows for immediate reinforcement. I usually follow this procedure for two to three days. Only after the final test do I collect the papers and correct them myself. By that time almost everyone has a perfect paper. The students are motivated because they see their own improvement right away, which can happen only when *they check their own papers,* and then they are eager to take the test again to see how much better they can do.

Another way to develop real interest in spelling is to encourage your students to work in pairs, to select their own trouble-making words, and to test each other. The proof of the success of any spelling program is when daily writing contains fewer errors. And though I stress the idea that one should not worry about spelling when writing, if one has become automatically concerned about spelling, he will find that his writing is more error-free.

Punctuation and grammar

The most reasonable way to teach these is to face problems when they arise in children's writing. As you read your students' work be on the lookout for evidence of specific needs in the areas of punctuation and grammar. When you find that many of your students are misusing quotation marks, or writing too many run-on sentences, or using certain words incorrectly, plan some lessons that will highlight these problems and provide practice in the use of the proper forms. It is even quite helpful to project students' papers with the aid of an opaque projector in order to see the actual problem as it exists in your room. The paper can be projected in such a way that names do not appear—they are not important at this point.

When you find errors that seem to be true only for an individual do not waste class time teaching a lesson. For example, this means that if only Tom does not know how to set off a series of items with commas, only Tom needs individual instruction, not the rest of the class.

One of the most effective ways to help a student improve his writing skills is to schedule individual conferences. These are not easy to fit in, and you may be able to schedule very few with any one student during the year, but the conference is a valuable asset to a writing program. You may need to give up some of your time before and after school for such conferences. Even the lunch period or during recess may be possibilities for you. If your children can work quietly at some worthwhile task, perhaps enjoying a library book, you can fit conferences in during the regular class hours. It may be that primary children can have learning experiences carried on in small groups by intermediate children, and for this time teachers of both classes can schedule some conferences. You may also find that you can divide your students into compatible pairs and then conduct conferences with two students at one time.

Whatever arrangement you can work out, you will find these meetings rewarding. During the conference you will discuss the ideas in a student's current writing, and through this personal discussion, the student will find he has new thoughts about which to write or new ways to express thoughts he already has formulated in his mind. Also during these conferences you should read aloud something the student has written and make pertinent comments regarding the problems of punctuation and grammar which you note. Finally, you should be able to guide students into new writing challenges as a result of these sessions.

Proofreading

Whenever I examine English textbooks for their suggestions on proofreading I find the same things emphasized: be sure every word is spelled correctly, check to see that you indented each paragraph, check for needed capital letters, be sure you have neat margins, etc. Never have I found the two most important questions that a writer must ask when proofreading:

1. Did I say what I meant to say?
2. Have I selected the most fitting words and phrases to say it?

If the writer decides the answer to both questions is negative, then who cares about capital letters and neat margins!

A suggestion about giving letter grades to creative writing

I would like to say that letter grades should not be given to something as personal as one's own writing. But realistically, I know that most of you are in a school system which demands grades in English. If you must grade the writing your students do, let them be involved in setting up the standards for assigning grades. Then try to collect at least four pieces of writing per week from every student, but do *not* grade them. Once every week or two, at the most, ask your students to re-read all they have written to date and select the one piece which is the best, the most representative, the one that comes closest to saying well what they wanted to say. Each student should then take that one piece of writing and check it over, re-write it as many times as he feels necessary, and finally hand it in to be graded. This seems to me to be the most equitable procedure for both student and teacher.

I make it a practice to send home a monthly publication entitled "Our Best Writing from the Month of _____." In this way parents share in the work of their children, and they can discover the variety of writing topics that occurs in the classroom as well as the variety in writing styles. I duplicate the writings, but I never copy spelling errors, for that can too easily be a serious source of embarrassment which diverts attention away from the essential aspect—the *message* in the composition.

The following are examples of writing that student authors chose as some of their best efforts:

In this one Mark felt he had been successful in painting a good word-picture for the reader.

THE BEAR HUNT

Yesterday we went bear hunting in Robinson Canyon where the old orchards are. We saw an old covered up mine shaft for about the fifteenth time, but it was uncovered about four or five feet down. I saw quite a few bear tracks but they were too old.

In the first orchard there was a pitch dark passageway with limbs hanging down in front of you and that made it scary.

Then we went to the next orchard by the pioneer settlement. We could not see a bear anywhere so we started to target practice. I was right next to Dad when he shot and I kept on hearing bells ringing.

On the way back I asked Dad if I could drive and he said, "If the road gets better." But it did not.

—Mark K.

In this poem Janice felt pleased with her effort at free verse.

SMALL

Small is a particle in the air.
Small is a leaf from a tree.
Small is a petal from a flower.
Small is a piece of chalk.
Small is a word.
Small is a star.
Small is a letter.
Small is a pebble.
Small is a strand of hair.
Small is a ladybug in the trees.
Small is a speck of dirt or dust.
Small can be a screw.
Small was me one time.
Small can be lots of things.
And that's the story of small.

—Janice H.

Occasionally we write about something that irritates us, and the challenge is to get the reader to feel the same irritation. Hanna was delighted with her piece.

NOISY THINGS MAKE ME MAD

Every night everything is quiet, but in the morning at six thirty my noisy alarm clock yawns and opens up his big fat mouth. Then I get up and stumble across the room. Push the button and stumble back to my nest. I grumble and mumble. Fifteen minutes later another alarm clock goes off. Then I get up. Wendy is so noisy that I wish I could tape her mouth. Thirty minutes later Wendy gets up. You never heard such a noise! Tramping of feet and dishes banging together. Finally it is off to school! The house gets a rest. Oh, dear! Here it comes again! First, the door opens, next it slams. Lunch boxes are dumped on the davino. The refrigerator opens, nothing there. Slam! Goes the door. On goes the box. Pretty soon the rest of the gang comes. Dinner is ready. Go wash your hands, Wendy! Off goes the box. That was a good dinner, Mom. Tom can unload the dishwasher and Peter can load it. On goes the box. Finally it is quiet again.

—Hanna W.

Patti taught me a most valuable lesson. Each time we began a writing period after my introductory efforts to motivate, I would find Patti sitting with a blank paper and staring into space. When I would ask if I could help her get started, her answer was, "No, I am just thinking about what I want to write and how to say it." The first time she said this I was quite suspicious as I did not know her very well yet. We teachers can feel so uncomfortable when a child is just sitting, not reading or writing! Soon I discovered that Patti always needed half of the period to organize her thoughts and then she would begin to write. Since this experience I now stress the value of taking time to think through what one is going to write. The following is an example of what a little serious thought can produce.

GENTLE

Gentle is a mother horse
That cares for her foal.
　Gentle is the night black,
Black as coal.
　Gentle is the wind
That blows a flower.
　Gentle is the rain
That makes a shower.
　Gentle are many things
That I cannot describe.
　Gentle were some that
Fought alone and died.

—Patti P.

Nancy's piece was the result of trying to write from another point of view. One child wrote as though he were a shoe, another as a fish, and Nancy became her cat.

MY CAT'S MORNING

I was sitting on the porch railing. Through the window I saw someone coming to the door. I pounced down and started pawing at the screen door. The door opened and I squeeked at the girl. She copied me and snatched me from the ground. Oh, my stomach. I squealed again and was copied. I was put down, dashed upstairs, turned the corner, saw a blanket which looked soft, so I jumped. My, I did not know it was this soft. I wonder what it is like inside. Mm, pretty nice. In fact, I like it. Hey, how do you get out of here? Oh, I see. I guess I will see if it works. Good, it does.

I guess I will walk around as long as I'm out. Hey, I'm slipping. Ouch, that hurt! I guess I will let everybody know I am hurt! "Howl." Heh, heh, someone is coming. Oh, oh, it is that girl. Oh, dear. Too late now. Grab!!! "Oh, are you all right?" Somehow, I think I felt better before she came. Finally, I thought she would never let me down. As long as I am free I guess I will go downstairs. Oh, great, I have to race her down the stairs. Charge!!! Well, at least I won. I think I will go to sleep. Purr. Purr.

—Nancy H.

IN SUMMARY

1. The technical skills of writing will have meaning, and thus be worth teaching, only when students have something to express and a desire to do so.
2. Proofreading is more than correcting errors; it is perfecting a piece of writing in terms of the ideas expressed.
3. Involve students in setting up criteria for evaluation and permit them to select what written works should be evaluated.
4. Individual conferences provide one of the best settings in which to help students grow in their written expression.

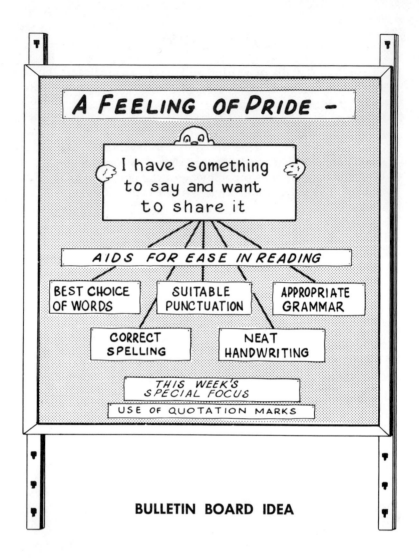

BULLETIN BOARD IDEA

COMMENT: This bulletin board can serve as a guide for effective proofreading. **THIS WEEK'S SPECIAL FOCUS** might include one of the general aids as listed above, but often it would be more specific, for instance: (1) use of quotation marks, (2) finding more vivid words to describe or express action, (3) avoiding run-on sentences.

14

Valuable Resources for the Teacher

NCTE—your professional organization

The National Council of Teachers of English is probably the single most valuable resource for an elementary teacher. Membership brings with it a yearly subscription to *Elementary English* (junior and senior high teachers receive *The English Journal,* and college instructors receive *College Composition* —though any member may arrange to receive all three journals). *Elementary English* is published eight times each year and contains articles on all areas of the language arts. Here one can find examples of other teachers' success in specific activities, pertinent research throughout the field of the language arts, in-depth studies of well-known authors of children's books, and reviews of new books for children. In addition to the professional journals, the Council publishes an extensive array of pamphlets and books related to all phases of the language arts.

Once each year, the week of Thanksgiving, a national convention is held in a major city. (There is a rotation schedule so that each geographical region has an opportunity to provide the host city.) This annual convention is exciting and highly stimulating for it is a time to share common problems with teachers and administrators from all over the country. It is also a time for intensive study in areas of special interest led by outstanding educators in the field. There usually are demonstrations with children, visits to observe innovative school programs, and small discussion groups composed both of famous names and of teachers from college, secondary, and elementary levels.

The conventions are well attended, but they need to be better represented by elementary teachers in order to improve the balance in the discussion and study groups. It is more difficult for teachers in the elementary schools to get away from their classrooms, but the rewards for both the individual and the school from which the teacher comes are worth whatever sacrifices need to be made.

For information regarding membership and lists of available publications write to:

> The National Council of Teachers of English
> 508 South Sixth Street
> Champaign, Illinois   61820

Files of all sorts

A poetry file will put at your finger tips the favorite poems you enjoy sharing with students. Even though a published anthology is possible, it will never contain all the poems you wish to have. One way to collect poems is to have on your desk a card file containing your favorite poems copied onto separate cards so that you can read them directly without referring to any books. The file can be organized into such categories as: holidays, seasons, sports, beauty, animals, poems for creative dramatizations, and poems for choral reading. There can be sections for different units of study which occur in your room. Instead of a filing box on the desk, some teachers prefer to have a loose-leaf notebook with dividers to aid in the organization of the poetry. The advantages of having either kind of poetry file include: (1) convenience in adding new poems whenever you happen on to those that appeal to you, and (2) ease in locating a specific poem when a moment in your teaching occurs that would be enriched by the use of it. This means that when you look up to see a sudden spring rain hitting the classroom windows, you can reach into your poetry file for your selections about rain. I remember my first year of teaching, when I had no poetry file, and my fourth-grade boys were playing softball with a passion. I knew "Casey at the Bat" would be ideal to share with them, but I had to spend many days hunting for that poem in various anthologies before I located it. How much more effective it would have been if I could have pulled it out *at the moment* it seemed most usable.

Another essential file is one of pictures. Pictures are extremely useful in making a room attractive, in providing stimulation for discussion, and for motivating creative writing. Old magazines, calendars, advertising brochures, and the newspapers are a few accessible sources for pictures. The pictures you collect should be neatly cut and carefully mounted on tagboard or heavier cardboard, preferably without borders for then you are free to vary the background colors from year to year when you wish to display certain pictures on a bulletin board. A picture file should also be organized into categories useful to you, perhaps similar to those you have developed for a poetry file. The container in which to store pictures must be quite large in order to accommodate the odd sizes of many pictures.

In using pictures to motivate creative writing make sure that children can easily view them. This means that if the whole class is to write from the inspiration of a single picture, it must be large enough and placed high enough for everyone to see. It is even more effective to distribute smaller pictures in order that each child may have one at his own desk as he writes. Sometimes these small pictures can be propped up on the chalk trays and then each child may come up to choose one that attracts him. The following is what one fifth grader felt when she selected a picture of an autumnal scene:

THE AUTUMN DAY

It was an autumn day. The sun was very bright. All was quiet in the pumpkin field. At this time of the year the pumpkins were gold in splendor. The workers of the field

had done their work for the day. The buckets were filled
to the brim. Then all of a sudden dusk had come. To all
the little animals in the forest nearby, the day had just
begun. The rabbits, squirrels, chipmunks, field mice, and
birds began to play. The squirrels, rabbits, and mice
started pushing over the buckets. The chipmunks scam-
pered about the fields joyfully. The birds began to sing
loudly. All this on an autumn day.

—Wendy W.

A third useful file is a collection of composition ideas. This
file should be available to students when they are at a loss for
an idea about which to write. In such a file there could be:

1. A section of unusual opening sentences.

    1) The stranger walked quietly to the rear of the station.
    2) When I am tired I just want to go somewhere and relax.
    3) Cold blowing snow forced me to keep moving.
    4) New friends are sometimes difficult to make.

2. A section of situations or titles.

    1) Choosing a new pet
    2) Getting lost
    3) Celebrating a happy occasion
    4) An opinion I have

Such a file of ideas could be added to each year by the students. In fact, some of them would enjoy thinking up new
ones. Each idea should be typed or written on a card and then
the students can help classify the different ideas.

One file that is especially useful to teachers is one in which
information regarding books for special purposes is kept. This
includes annotations of books that are good to read aloud,
books that children like to read to themselves, and annotations
for professional books and articles that the teacher uses at various times during the year.

Other materials you need
in the classroom

Ideally every child will have a dictionary at his desk. He
should discover what a friend the dictionary can be, for it will

define words, show how they are used in simple sentences, and offer aid in pronunciation. And students need to observe you referring to a dictionary in your daily work. A classroom should also include a standard "adult" dictionary, a rhyming dictionary, and a thesaurus.

Some basic art materials should be handy for illustrating stories, designing book covers, and creating favorite scenes from library books. Minimum materials are: manila paper, colored construction paper, crayons, tempera and watercolor paints, glue, and scissors.

A record player and a collection of records will be an asset for stimulating ideas and for providing background music while the children are working. Try for a variety of musical selections from classical to very modern jazz, from choral to solo voices, from orchestral to band music.

Bulletin boards and interest centers are essential to a classroom where the language arts serve as the major focus of the curriculum. Throughout this book there have been ideas for bulletin boards related to the subject matter of each chapter. A bulletin board should be functional—it should catch a child's attention and encourage him to *do* something. Most displays need to be changed about every two or three weeks. In fact, at the end of each week, you should look about the room and ask yourself: when was the last time the children or I made reference to each bulletin board? If you find that no one needed the board during the week then it is time for a change. Bulletin boards must be functional and not merely serve as decorative wall covering.

Annotated bibliography

The following materials can be quite useful for a teacher who wants to become more creative in his teaching of the language arts. Where an entry does not include an annotation there is a reference to the chapter where the book is described:

AMIDON, EDMUND J., and NED A. FLANDERS, *The Role of the Teacher in the Classroom*. See Chapter 3.

ANDERSON, PAUL S., *Language Skills in Elementary Education*. New

York: Macmillan Company, 1964. A comprehensive text for both experienced and beginning teachers.

ANDERSON, VERNA DIEKMAN, PAUL S. ANDERSON, FRANCIS BALLANTINE, and VIRGIL HOWES, *Reading in the Language Arts* (2nd ed.). New York: Macmillan Company, 1968. Quite useful as it includes the writings of so many experts in the field.

APPLEGATE, MAUREE, *Easy in English*. Evanston, Illinois: Row, Peterson and Company, 1960. A book loaded with enthusiasm and practical suggestions to the teacher who wishes to excite children about language.

ARBUTHNOT, MAY HILL, *Children and Books*. Chicago: Scott, Foresman and Company. See Chapter 6.

———, *Time for Poetry*. Chicago: Scott, Foresman and Company. See Chapter 6.

Bulletin for the Center for Children's Books. University of Chicago Press. See Chapter 1.

BURROWS, ALVINA TREUT, DORIS C. JACKSON, and DOROTHY O. SAUNDERS, *They All Want to Write* (3rd ed.). New York: Holt, Rinehart and Winston, 1964. A book of practical suggestions accompanied by numerous examples of writing by children.

DAWSON, MILDRED, editor. *Children, Books and Reading*. Newark, Delaware: International Reading Association, 1964. Includes these articles: "Striking the Spark," "The Right Book," "The School's Influence," and "A Comprehensive Literature Program." Paperback.

DIXON, JOHN, *Growth Through English*. Champaign, Illinois: National Council of Teachers of English, 1967. A report based upon the Dartmouth Seminar of 1966. Mr. Dixon makes a convincing case that the primary purpose in language is to share experience. There is an analysis of language activities in the classroom. Paperback.

DUKER, SAM, *Listening: Readings*. New York: The Scarecrow Press, 1966. See Chapter 7.

FENWICK, SARA INNIS, editor, *A Critical Approach to Children's Literature*. University of Chicago Press, 1967. Papers presented at the thirty-first annual conference of the Graduate Library School, August 1-3, 1966. Stimulating articles including these titles: "Children's Reading and Adult Values," "Psychological Significance of Children's Literature," "Literature for 'Children Without,'" and "Current Reviewing of Children's Books."

FLOYD, WILLIAM D., "An Analysis of the Oral Questioning Activity in Selected Colorado Primary Classrooms." Unpublished Ed.D. dissertation, Colorado State College, Greeley, 1961. See Chapter 3.

FRAZIER, ALEXANDER, editor, *New Directions in Elementary English*. Champaign, Illinois: National Council of Teachers of English,

1967. Papers collected from the 1966 Spring Institutes of the elementary language arts of the NCTE. Presents a revealing look at the future of the studies of literature, language, and composition in our schools. Paperback.

GARRISON, WEBB B., *Why You Say It: The Fascinating Stories Behind Over 700 Everyday Words and Phrases.* New York: Abington Press, 1955. See Chapter 8.

GLAUS, MARLENE, *From Thoughts to Words.* Champaign, Illinois: National Council of Teachers of English, 1965. See Chapter 8.

HOLBROOK, DAVID, *Children's Writing.* Cambridge University Press, 1967. An examination of many examples of children's writing with comments and thought-provoking questions which are directed to the teacher who is seeking to improve his writing assignments. Paperback.

The Horn Book. Boston, Massachusetts. See Chapter 1.

HUCK, CHARLOTTE S., and DORIS YOUNG KUHN, *Children's Literature in the Elementary School* (2nd ed.). New York: Holt, Rinehart and Winston, Inc., 1968. One of the best comprehensive treatments of this broad field.

LAIRD, HELENE and CHARLTON, *The Tree of Language.* Cleveland: World Publishing Company, 1957. See Chapter 8.

LANE, S. M., and M. KEMP, *An Approach to Creative Writing in the Primary School.* London: Blackie, 1967. A refreshing and stimulating book written for teachers in England of elementary school aged children with such chapters as, "The use of music," "The use of pictures," and "Using the environment."

MACKINTOSH, HELEN K., editorial chairman, *Children and Oral Language.* A joint statement of the Association for Childhood Education International, the Association for Supervision and Curriculum Development, the International Reading Association, and the National Council of Teachers of English, 1964. A brief pamphlet but amazingly comprehensive in dealing with the research, classroom practices, evaluation, and needed action in the often neglected area of oral language.

MARTIN, BILL, JR., *The Human Connection.* Washington, D.C.: Department of Elementary-Kindergarten-Nursery Education, National Education Association of the United States, 1967. A sensitively convincing story of a teacher who learns that language and experience are the human connection with such unique ideas as "a field trip is a language laboratory." Pamphlet.

MULLER, HERBERT, *The Uses of English.* New York: Holt, Rinehart and Winston, Inc., 1967. Guidelines for the teaching of English from the Anglo-American Conference at Dartmouth College. Challenging proposals for the creative teacher.

MUNKRES, ALBERTA, *Helping Children in Oral Communication.* New York: Teachers College, Columbia University, 1959. A collection of examples of children talking, captured by tape recorder with helpful comments for the teacher who wishes to aid children in the art of talking. Paperback.

National Council of Teachers of English, "Development of Taste in Literature." Champaign, Illinois: NCTE, 1962-63. Four excellent articles reprinted from *Elementary English* and *English Journal* by Nila B. Smith, Helen Huus, Leonard W. Joll, and Angela M. Broening.

RUSSELL, DAVID H., and ELIZABETH F. RUSSELL, *Listening Aids Through the Grades*. New York: Teachers College, Columbia University, 1959. See Chapter 7.

SANDERS, NORRIS M., *Classroom Questions: What Kinds?* New York: Harper and Row, 1966. See Chapter 3.

Saturday Review, New York. Section on children's books, Zena Sutherland, editor. See bibliography, Chapter 1.

SEBASTA, SAM LEATON, *Ivory, Apes and Peacocks: The Literature Point of View*, Vol. 12, Part 2. International Reading Association, 1968. Proceedings of the twelfth annual convention. A stimulating collection of papers on techniques, programs, appreciation, and selection.

SHUY, ROGER W., *Discovering American Dialects*. Champaign, Illinois: National Council of Teachers of English, 1967. See Chapter 4.

SIKS, GERALDINE, and HAZEL DUNNINGTON, editors, *Children's Theater and Creative Dramatics*. Seattle: University of Washington Press, 1961. See Chapter 2.

SIKS, GERALDINE BRAIN, *Creative Dramatics*. New York: Harper and Row, 1958. See Chapter 2.

———, *Children's Literature for Dramatization: An Anthology*. New York: Harper and Row, 1964. See Chapter 2.

SMITH, LILLIAN H., *The Unreluctant Years: A Critical Approach to Children's Literature*. New York: Viking Press, 1967. A perceptively presented case for children's literature and the need to subject it to the same standards of criticism of any form of literature, published in paperback by arrangement with the American Library Association who first printed it in hard cover in 1953.

WAGNER, GUY, MAX HOSIER, and MILDRED BLACKMAN, *Listening Games: Building Listening Skills with Instructional Games*. Darien, Connecticut: Grade Teacher Publications, 1962. See Chapter 7.

WALMSTROM, JEAN, and ANNABEL ASHLEY, *Dialects: U.S.A.* Champaign, Illinois: National Council of Teachers of English, 1963. See Chapter 4.

WALTER, NINA WILLIS, *Let Them Write Poetry*. New York: Holt, Rinehart and Winston, Inc., 1962. See Chapter 10.

WARD, WINIFRED, *Playmaking with Children* (2nd ed.). New York: Appleton-Century Crofts, Inc., 1957. See Chapter 2.

Suggested list to send home to parents who want ideas about books to read aloud

The following books are especially suited for reading aloud, and they are books that adults should enjoy reading to their children. You could duplicate this list, or parts of it, and send it home with the children. Such a list is quite useful to parents early in the school year or close to the Christmas season. Books marked with a *P* are best for reading to children up through third grade; those marked with an *I* are best for children in grades four, five, six, and seven; the asterisk * indicates books that should have an especial appeal to various minority groups.

I *Doctor's Boy,* Karin Anckarsvard. Translated from the Swedish by Annabelle Macmillan. Illustrated by Fermin Rocker. New York: Harcourt, Brace & World, Inc., 1965. Young boy accompanies his father on his medical calls early in the century in Sweden.

I *The Nightingale,* Hans Christian Andersen. Translated by Eva LeGallienne. Illustrated by Nancy Burkert. New York: Harper and Row, Publishers, 1965. Exquisite double-page pictures in full color.

P *How Babies Are Made,* Andrew C. Andry and Steven Schepp. Illustrated by Blake Hampton. New York: Time-Life, 1968. To be used by adults and children *together.* Illustrations are photographs of colored paper sculpture. They are quite explicit.

I *The Big Sea,* Richard Armstrong. New York: David McKay, Inc., 1965. Exciting sea adventure.

I *Norse Gods and Giants,* Ingri and Edgar Parin D'Aulaire. New York: Doubleday & Company, Inc., 1967. Handsomely illustrated Norse myths.

I* *Walk the World's Rim,* Betty Baker. New York: Harper and Row, Publishers, 1965. A search for gold by three 16th-century Spaniards, their Negro slave Esteban, and a young Indian boy.

I *The Faraway Lurs,* Harry Behn. Cleveland: The World Publishing Company, 1963. A gentle love story set in Denmark during the Bronze Age.

I* *The Two Uncles of Pablo,* Harry Behn. Illustrated by Mel Silverman. New York: Harcourt, Brace & World, Inc., 1959. A book with humor and excellent characterizations.

I* *Backbone of the King,* Marcia Brown. New York: Charles

Scribner's Sons, 1966. A hero tale from Hawaiian folk literature.

I   *Renfroe's Christmas,* Robert Burch. Illustrated by Rocco Negri.
New York: The Viking Press, Inc., 1968. A merry, yet touching
family story in a rural setting.

P   *Fortunately,* written and illustrated by Remy Charlip. New
York: *Parents' Magazine,* 1964. Delightfully humorous.

I   *The Big Road,* Tom E. Clarke. New York: Lothrop Lee &
Shepard Co., Inc., 1965. Depression era novel of 17-year-old
boy who tries to leave his farm life and a stepfather. Takes
place in the Pacific Northwest.

P   *Ramona the Pest,* Beverly Cleary. Illustrated by Louis Darling.
New York: William Morrow & Co., Inc., 1968. Five years old,
just entering kindergarten. A charming, humorous book.

I*   *Dead End School,* Robert Coles. Illustrated by Norman Rock-
well. Boston: Little, Brown & Co., 1968. Crowded school in
the ghetto. What happens when Jim moves to an uncrowded
school in an all-white neighborhood.

P   *The Fish from Japan,* Elizabeth Cooper. Illustrated by Beth
and Joe Krush. New York: Harcourt, Brace & World, Inc.,
1969. A boy brags at school that he is getting a fish in the mail.
When it comes it is a kite, so he uses his imagination.

P   *The Long and Dangerous Journey,* M. Jean Craig. Illustrated
by Ilb Ohlsson. New York: W. W. Norton & Company, Inc.,
1965. Mark's imagination changes an ordinary walk into quite
a dangerous trip. Lots of fun.

I   *Charley and the Chocolate Factory,* Roald Dahl. Illustrated
by Joseph Schindelman. New York: Alfred A. Knopf, Inc.,
1964. Very funny all the way.

I   *Journey from Peppermint Street,* Meindert De Jong. Pictures
by Emily McCully. New York: Harper & Row, Publishers, 1968.
Engrossing story of a boy who accompanies his grandfather on
a long walk inland to visit an aunt. Takes place in Holland in
the early 1900's.

I   *The Twenty-One Balloons,* written and illustrated by William
Pène Du Bois. New York: The Viking Press, Inc., 1947. An
amazing voyage of a professor who started out from San Fran-
cisco in one balloon and three weeks later was found in the
Atlantic with 20!

P   *Going Barefoot,* Aileen Fisher. Illustrated by Adrienne Adams.
New York: Thomas Y. Crowell Company, 1960. Poetry. Attractively illustrated. Makes one want to kick off his shoes.

I   *Gull Number 737,* Jean George. New York: Thomas Y. Crowell
Company, 1964. Perceptive characterizations. Scientific details
are vivid. Family relationships, particularly between father and
son, are sympathetically drawn.

I*   *The House of Dies Drear,* Virginia Hamilton. Illustrated by Eros Keith. New York: The Macmillan Company, 1968. Contemporary story of a Negro family who moves into a house formerly used in the Underground Railroad in Ohio. Dramatic story in an atmosphere of fear and danger.

I   *The Endless Steppe,* Esther Hautzig. New York: Thomas Y. Crowell Company, 1968. True story of a family forced to leave Poland in 1941 to live five arduous years in Russian Siberia.

P   *Bedtime for Frances,* Russell C. Hoban. Illustrated by Garth Williams. New York: Harper & Row, Publishers, 1960. Engaging picture book about a badger family and how young Frances forestalls going to sleep.

I   *Akavak; An Eskimo Journey,* written and illustrated by James Houston. New York: Harcourt, Brace & World, Inc., 1968. A rugged tale of determination and danger.

I   *The Wild Swans Fly,* Pauline B. Innis. New York: David McKay Co., Inc., 1964. A family of swans who become separated. The incidents are based on real observations.

I   *The Paleface Redskins,* written and illustrated by Jacqueline Jackson. Boston: Little, Brown & Co., 1958. A rousing story of four children who are again vacationing at a Wisconsin lake. They are intrigued by Indian lore and much distressed to find a new Scout camp built near by.

P*   *John Henry,* written and illustrated by Ezra Jack Keats. New York: Pantheon Books, Inc., 1965. Handsomely illustrated, this is the retelling of a favorite American legend.

I   *Jennifer, Hecate, Macbeth, William McKinley, and Me, Elizabeth,* written and illustrated by E. L. Konigsburg. New York: Atheneum Publishers, 1967. A very lonely girl and her seeming brush with witchcraft. Takes place in modern, suburban New York City.

I   *Lois Lenski's Christmas Stories,* written and illustrated by Lois Lenski. Philadelphia: J. B. Lippincott Co., 1968. A collection of stories and poems with a great variety in locale, time, and economic focus.

P*   *The Rooftop Mystery,* Joan M. Lexau. Illustrated by Syd Hoff. New York: Harper & Row, Publishers, 1968. An appealing book designed for the beginning reader.

P   *Tico and the Golden Wings,* written and illustrated by Leo Lionni. New York: Pantheon Books, Inc., 1964. Beautifully illustrated story of a bird who learns to use a remarkable gift to enrich the lives of others.

I   *Home from Far,* Jean Little. Illustrated by Jerry Lazare. Boston: Little, Brown & Co., 1965. Moving account of a family facing the death of a twin in an accident and the advent of two foster children.

P   *Burt Dow, Deep-Water Man,* written and illustrated by Robert McCloskey. New York: The Viking Press, Inc., 1963. Wildly illustrated story of an old fisherman who puts out to sea in his leaky boat and finally must escape from the belly of a whale.

I*   *Indian Annie: Kiowa Captive,* Alice Lee Marriot. New York: David McKay Co., Inc., 1965. Compelling story of a girl stolen by Indians who comes to love her Indian foster-parents dearly but finally must decide between marrying the Indian she loves or returning to her real parents.

I   *Stranger on Big Hickory,* Stephen Meader. Illustrated by Don Lambo. New York: Harcourt, Brace & World, Inc., 1964. A boy's 4-H project leads into a mystery about someone doing illegal trapping in the Pennsylvania countryside.

P*   *Mississippi Possum,* Miska Miles. Illustrated by John Schoenherr. Boston: Little, Brown & Co., 1965. A possum becomes tame when the river floods and forces him to come in contact with people.

I*   *Berries Goodman,* Emily Neville. New York: Harper & Row, Publishers, 1965. A move from New York City to the suburbs brings a boy into his first friendship with a Jewish boy and a first experience with prejudice.

I*   *Island of the Blue Dolphins,* Scott O'Dell. Boston: Houghton Mifflin Company, 1960. In the early 1800's an Indian girl survives 18 lonely years on an island off the California coast.

P   *Randy's Dandy Lions,* written and illustrated by Bill Peet. Boston: Houghton Mifflin Company, 1964. A delightfully silly book about a circus lion act that was a flop because of the lions' shyness.

P   *Tony's Birds,* Millicent Selsam. Illustrated by Kurt Werth. New York: Harper & Row, Publishers, 1961. An excellent beginning science book about a boy and his father who learn about birdwatching.

I   *The Day of the Bear,* Nancy Spofford. Chicago: Follett Publishing Company, 1964. A boy's first hunting trip. A perceptive view of a boy's sense of values. Takes place in central Florida.

I*   *Wayah of the Real People,* William O. Steele. Illustrated by Isa Barnett. New York: Holt, Rinehart & Winston, Inc., 1964. A Cherokee boy's year of schooling in colonial Williamsburg.

I*   *The Jazz Man,* Mary Hays Weik. Illustrated by Ann Grifalconi. New York: Atheneum Publishers, 1966. A boy in Harlem who seldom goes out because one leg is shorter than the other. Real trouble comes when the boy's mother leaves.

P   *Saucy,* Martha Welch. Illustrated by Unada. New York: Coward-McCann, Inc., 1968. When the dog is about to have puppies it disappears. Eventually the entire neighborhood joins in the search.

I   *The Moonball*, Ursula Moray Williams. Illustrated by Jane Paton. New York: Meredith Corporation, 1967. A fantasy with humor and perceptive characterization.

I   *Keefer's Landing*, Robert J. Willis. Chicago: Follett Publishing Company, 1964. A new highway threatens financial crisis. Well-written family story.

I   *Odyssey of Courage*, Maia Wojciechowska. New York: Atheneum Publishers, 1965. The dramatic story of Cabeza de Vaca who penetrated the unknown land from Florida to Mexico in the 16th century.

I*   *Amos Fortune: Freeman*, Elizabeth Yates. Illustrated by Nora S. Unwin. New York: Aladdin, 1950. Biography of a Negro, born in Africa, brought to this country as a slave, who became a most respected member of the community.

Index